Enterprise IoT

A Definitive Handbook

By Naveen Balani

Enterprise IoT

A Definite Handbook

By Naveen Balani (http://naveenbalani.com)

October 2015: First edition

January 2016: Second Edition

March 2016: Third Edition

Last Updated: 7th March 2016

Technical Editor: Rajeev Hathi

Cover Designer: Shao-Chun Wang@123rf.com

Introduction

Internet of Things (IoT) is one of the most hyped concepts in today's technology world. However, with so much hype, there is still a lot of confusion on what does Internet of Things actually mean and what it takes to build IoT applications and how to apply it in various industries.

There exist many definitions on "Internet of Things" and even getting on to the same terminology and definition seems difficult nowadays. We have seen multiple definitions over a period of time, such as 'Internet of Everything', 'Internet of Food', 'Internet of your Things', 'Internet of People' and the list goes on. They all mean the same, so let's start with a simple definition of Internet of Things.

"Internet of Things is a vision where every object in the world has the potential to connect to the Internet and provide their data so as to derive actionable insights on its own or through other connected objects"

The object can be anything – a vehicle, machinery, airport, city, people, phone or even a shoe. From a connected vehicle solution, you can understand the driver behaviour and vehicle usage patterns, from a connected machines solution you can determine when do machines need servicing, from a connected airport solution you can understand many things like - how much time the passenger needs to wait for check-in and security, from an operational perspective it could help to optimize the passenger movement and ensure the right equipments are available at the right time to ensure quick serviceability and finally say, from a connected footwear solution you can understand how much you have run so far and your app can automatically purchase a new pair of shoes based on the remaining shoe life.

As we can see, it's not just about connectivity, but how to use the connected data in context of your application or for that matter other connected solutions to derive insights which can't be uncovered before. Today we are seeing data (both structured and unstructured) growing by leaps and bounds available through mediums like blogs, social media, transactional systems, etc. With advent of IoT, you will see a large volume of raw data emitting from devices like sensors. Such huge and complex set of data, if not attended to, can go wasted and opportunity lost in terms of building a smart environment around us. It has become increasingly important to process this data both in batches and real-time, apply correlations, derive insights and predict outcomes through appropriate analysis.

Today we are living in the world of disruptive technologies where every kind of technology is connected to form a solution. IoT is no exception. With over 100+ vendors providing 100+ devices, services and platforms to build IoT applications, and plus we have existing systems having already employed some connectivity and automation, like manufacturing plants, it is going to take a huge effort in making these vibrant heterogeneous environment of devices talk to each other. While focusing on the issue of addressing this web of complexity, understanding the real benefit of IoT and most importantly how to get started on IoT is lost..

In this book, our focus will be to provide a clear vision on Internet of Things and everything you should know to get started on applying and building Enterprise IoT applications in any industry. The concepts listed in the book are applicable across industries. Till date, it's difficult to find a single perspective of what does an Enterprise IoT stack actually mean and our intent is to provide an applicability guide that can be taken as reference for building any IoT application.

In the course of the book, we would describe some of the key components of Internet of Things through our Enterprise IoT stack. We would look at how to incrementally apply IoT transformations to build connected solutions in various industries. At the end, we would understand the technical strategy and how to build IoT applications using IoT cloud offerings from Microsoft, IBM, Amazon and GE Predix and even build one using open source technologies.

To summarize, as part of the book we would cover the following -

- A detailed overview of key components of Internet of Things and the most comprehensive view of an Enterprise IoT stack.
- How to apply IoT in context of real world applications by covering detailed use cases on manufacturing, automotive and home automation.
- Understand the technical strategy and how to implement IoT applications using Microsoft, IBM, Amazon and GE Predix IoT offerings and various open source technologies and map it to our Enterprise IoT stack.

For any comments, suggestions or queries please reach us at http://www.enterpriseiotbook.com or email me at me@naveenbalani.com

Chapter 1. Enterprise IoT Stack

In order to realize and build Enterprise IoT applications, we first need to understand the key components, requirements and complexity that go into building end to end IoT solutions.

An Enterprise IoT stack is a set of core capabilities and services that enable us to build IoT applications. In this chapter, we would walk through each component of an Enterprise IoT stack in detail, talk about the current challenges and how these components interact with each other.

The Enterprise IoT stack is later used as a reference to map the IoT services provided by leading commercial cloud offerings. Our intent in this chapter is to provide a first applicability stack that can be considered as a reference for building any IoT application along with leveraging commercial or open source technologies.

IoT Stack

Solutions	CONSUMER APPS (Home, Lifestyle ,Home, Mobility etc)	INDUSTRIAL APPS (Manufacturing, Building, Infrastructure, Energy etc)	IoT Security & Management
Cognitive Platform	INTERACTIONS (SPOKEN,GESTURES) INSTANT LEARNING COGNITIVE		Application Management Service Management
Analytics Platform	SERVICES (GEOSPATIAL etc) ACTIONABLE INSIGHTS (EVENTS & REPORTING) MACHINE LEARNING STREAM PROCESSING		Authorization Authentication
Core Platform	DATA STORAGE, DATA AGRREGRATION/ FILTER IOT MESSAGING MIDDLEWARE PROTOCOL GATEWAY		Simulation Device Security
Communication Protocols	MQTT, COAPP, DDS, XAMP... IPV5, IPV6, 6LOWPAN BLUETOOTH, GSM, ZIGBEE, MODBUS,BACNET		Device Management Deployment
Devices	DEVICES & COMPONENTS -Smart Devices -- Sensors / Actuators -- Embedded Devices		Firmware/ Code updates

The IoT stack comprises of many layers, starting with devices which communicate and send data to a core platform layer through different protocols based on the communication strategy. The core platform provides a set of key services to allow the devices to connect securely, store and replicate the data for fault tolerance and provide scalable technologies to accommodate millions of connected devices when required. Once the data is made available, the Analytics platform layer lets you analyze large volumes of data in real-time and batch/offline mode and discover actionable insights. The cognitive layer allows connected products to learn from behaviour and insights and provide a natural extension to one's digital life. On the top of the stack, we have the solutions layer which provides end to end consumer or industrial IoT applications, developed using the various stack services. We would explain all these concepts in detail in the course of this chapter.

The IoT stack should also address security and management of IoT applications. The requirements include device management, device security, secured bi-directional communication between devices and IoT platform, application security, network topologies, service management aspects, deployment and simulation.

Let's start with our first layer.

Device Layer

Devices are the 'things' of Internet of Things. Every device around us has a potential to connect to internet and give us some useful information. Types and categories of such devices are increasing as more and more industries are embracing the concept of IoT. So what kind of devices can fit the scheme of things? They are termed embedded devices which are equipped to read, process and send information over the internet. Embedded device has a chip or a circuitry called microcontroller that has all the necessary ingredients to power or control the device. Ingredients typically include a memory chip, an embedded processor, IO and network ports, etc. It may also have a small OS running Linux that enables us to drive the device. The ability to control the device and make it talk to the network is one of key aspects in IoT.

Price of computing resources have fallen down dramatically in recent years and therefore it has become very cheap to build controller boards and circuitry that drive our computing needs. These boards therefore can be envisioned to embed in any object around us to make it a more real-time talking object. The object can emit data about itself. Instances of embedded devices include but not limited to: sensors, gateways, mobile phones and tablets, personal gadgets, home automation devices, gateways, printers, healthcare industry devices like glucometer, heart rate and BP monitors, imaging systems, fitness bands, emergency response systems, medication reminder device, voice devices signalling a condition etc.. Also included are automotive industry devices like tire pressure monitor or a bigger concept like connected cars to drive road safety measures, supply chain industry devices like RFID reader and tags that enable efficient tracking of inventory during distribution, energy and utilities industry devices like smart grids, smart meters that helps monitoring and load balancing energy utilization, home automation industry devices like thermostat, home cam, smoke alarm, connected door lock etc.

Sensors

Sensors are devices that detect events and read changes in its environment, be it rotation and vibrations from machines, motion detection or temperature readings. Sensors play a very prominent role in the making of IoT as it can be programmed to sense the required environmental parameters that need to be monitored and convert them into meaningful data. Sensors by itself do not have input and output control or functions. The sensed information can be viewed in a console connected to another device like desktop or mobile.

Sensors come in connected form and a single form. Connected sensors are network of sensor nodes that capture information from the physical object or resource within a particular area and send it across over the network. For example, a collection of smart water sensors that measure quality of water and indicate pollution levels by sensing different polluting ingredients in the water. A single sensor is a standalone device that emits signals based on the target object's movement. It could be also as simple as making an alert beep at regular intervals. For example, a medicine bottle may have a sensor that alerts with a beep to indicate the patient that it is now the time to take the medicine. Sensors may or may not be instructed. For instance, some sensors may be instructed to control its behaviour through low level programming API. Information from the sensor is transmitted via a device gateway. Some sensors may have a capability to directly transmit the information to the internet. Sensors are low powered device and often equipped with a small longer life battery that runs for months or even years. Some sensors are even powered using solar energy.

Actuators
Actuators are devices that act with the physical world based on the input received and carry out the required action. The action can be a motion, lighting, emitting sound, controlling power etc. An example would be the connected door locks, which can be controlled (locked or unlocked) using remote control device and actuator being responsible for controlling the movement of the lock motor.

Tagged devices or objects
Radio Frequency Identification (RFID) tags are smart bar codes that identifies the device or a product and works in conjunction with the RFID reader to track the product information and send it across the network. These tags are attached to the products and the reader scans the tag and extracts the product information and sends the data over the network or the cloud which can be then further analyzed in real-time or offline. The concept also works on radio frequencies. Manufacturing, retail and supply chain industries have long started using this concept. Even in automotive industry, vehicles are tracked with RFID during the inspection process. The concept is also making its mark in aviation and healthcare and many more industries.

Near Field Communication (NFC) enables devices to communicate with each other over shorter radio frequencies. It works more like RFID, but the device with NFC protocol can act both as a reader and a tag and therefore it can also be used as a two way communication. The ideal use case for NFC is the contactless payment where one can use a NFC enabled Smartphone and tap it to the payment terminal device to make the payment. Your card details are securely stored in the mobile and read by the payment terminal device. Both your Smartphone and the payment terminal uses NFC to communicate with each other.

Beacons are another form of tagged devices that transmit signals or broadcast its location information using Bluetooth LE to the nearby Bluetooth enabled device. A smartphone can detect the beacon device and trigger an application to perform some contextual function. For example, you enter a retail store with a beacon installed denim department and your smartphone detects the beacon signal and launches a beacon enabled app that shows you the list of jeans brands available in the department. The communication happens on low radio frequency using Bluetooth LE or Smart Bluetooth that consumes less energy.

Devices for prototyping

Apart from real life industry devices, there also exists devices to prototype or test your IoT use cases. These are controller boards itself. Some of such known devices are Arduino, Raspberry Pi, Intel Galileo, BeagleBone etc. Using these boards you can create a small prototype to demonstrate the working of IoT sitting at home. The board enables you to connect to different sensors and actuators and provides network ports for internet connectivity. The ready availability of these devices makes it an ideal choice of prototyping, but these devices can also be used to build commercial connected products.

Communication Layer

The device layer earlier discussed different types of devices with different networking abilities. Devices will communicate with communication layer to set up network connectivity and send the data to the Internet. This section will feature different communication strategies that one can use based on the available device. We will also discuss different communication protocols.

Communication Strategy

The section discusses different communication strategies that can be used with IoT devices. It will depict how devices will communicate with the Internet to transmit or send data. The communication strategy is devised based on the networking capability of each device. Talking about device networking capability, hosts of IoT devices by itself are unable to route data directly to the internet due to protocol incompatibility. Though there are some that may be able to directly connect with the Internet. Devices that are unable to connect directly to Internet make use of something called 'gateway' or a 'hub'. We will talk about device gateway in detail in next section.

Device Gateway

An IoT Device gateway is a device that glues or connects incompatible networks or protocols and provides a means to connect devices to the internet. Low powered devices like sensors connect to a gateway through protocols like Z-wave or Bluetooth LE protocol, which in turn will communicate with the broadband router to route the messages to the internet. A broadband router could use WLAN or WI-FI to connect to internet. Protocols like ZigBee or Z-wave by itself are not equipped or capable of talking to the internet directly and therefore gateway device is used. The gateway will translate the incoming ZigBee data into IP data that can be then routed to the internet. Gateways can also act like a firewall thereby securing the devices from any malicious attack.

Smart Gateway

We could also have something called as 'smart' gateways. Such gateways have their own local storage and embedded application to perform analytics on data streamed directly from the devices. These are also called edge gateways. They are configured right at the edge of the device so that the data need not be sent over the network to the internet and can be analyzed or filtered close to the device in the gateway itself. The concept is also called 'fog computing' - a term devised by Cisco. The benefits of edge gateways lie in reduced network traffic and bandwidth, increased efficiency in terms of core data processing and delivering real -time processing.

Tip – Eclipse Kura is an open source project that provides a platform for building IoT edge gateways. It is a smart application container that enables remote management of such gateways and provides a wide range of APIs for allowing you to write and deploy your own IoT application. We would revisit Kura in Chapter 3.

Smartphone as a gateway

Another form of communication could be through the use of smartphones. Instead of gateway, a device can talk to a smartphone through say Bluetooth protocol and the data can be then channelized to the cellular network through a SIM card. This way a Smartphone can act as a gateway and eliminates the need of having a dedicated gateway device or a broadband router. A limitation to this approach is that smartphone by itself will not automate the process of data communication from the device to the internet. A manual intervention is required to set up the process of communication, for instance launching the corresponding application on the phone.

Direct connectivity

Certain devices have the capability to directly connect to the Internet without the need of any gateway. It could be either through Wi-Fi or cellular network. Modern day microcontrollers are equipped with Wi-Fi capability that enables devices to broadcast itself over the internet. The obvious advantage is that there is no need for any dedicated gateway thereby saving that one extra hop to send the data to the cloud or internet.

Device-to-device

Another form is a device-to-device communication. This form of communication defers the process of relaying data to the internet. Devices communicate with each other to form a mesh network. Devices communicate to collect information, report their existing states, send alerts or perform discovery routines. The communication could be with or without the human intervention. For example, a home security system may connect with a nearby alarm system to alert if someone approaches a door. The alert then can be sent to the internet so that if you are outside the home, you can get the status update.

API Connectivity

API based communication is the new talk of the town. In this approach, devices communicate its state to an internet service provider (say A) which then uses an API (often a REST URL) to communicate to another service provider (say B) which then triggers action to another device. This kind of API-based communication eliminates the need of installing a shared gateway. This mode of communication is handy when there are multiple disparate devices associated with a vendor service that needs to shake hands to realize a use case.

Communication protocols
Communication protocol is responsible for network connectivity. In the parlance of IoT, we will define two forms of communication protocols, one that provides direct Internet connectivity and another that requires some form of gateway to route the data to the Internet. Let's first look at the protocols that enable us to connect directly with the Internet. The following diagram shows a typical IoT communication model.

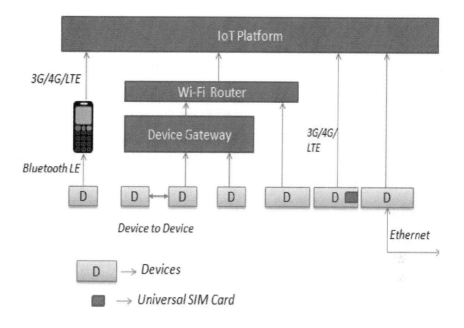

Wi-Fi

Wi-Fi protocol needs no introduction; we can't imagine a world without Wi-Fi. With Wi-Fi protocol, you can connect any device securely to a Wi-Fi gateway using security options supported by the gateway. Wi-Fi devices consumes a lot of power and may not be a good option when it comes to connecting small constrained devices as it can quickly become an overhead for these devices. There arises a need to create a standard like Wi-Fi protocol which makes it easier to discover and connect devices seamlessly with the IoT network. Hopefully, in future, we would have new standardized protocols like Wi-Fi which caters to requirements like low power consumption, longer battery life, etc. for connected products.

Ethernet

Ethernet provides a wired option where devices need to be physically connected to communicate over the network. This option might work for connected solutions like home/office, where devices are generally fixed, but this is not an option for most of the IoT applications, as it makes devices immovable.

Tip - LoRaWAN (Long Range Wide Area Network) is the latest addition to the new set of protocols to address the unique requirements for IoT. It is optimized for low power consumption and to support large networks with millions and millions of devices. The LoRa® Alliance @ https://www.lora-alliance.org/ plans to standardize the Low Power Wide Area Networks being deployed around the world to enable Internet of Things application.

Cellular

Cellular communication protocols include the connectivity options like 2G, 3G, 4G, LTE, etc. that your phone uses to connect to the cellular network. Similar to phones, this requires a data subscription package from a cellular network provider. From an IoT perspective, a device should not solely depend on cellular protocol but also allow itself to connect to other protocols like Bluetooth LE or Wi-Fi, so as to use existing connectivity options wherever available.

The second form of communication protocols requires a gateway to translate device specific commands into IP equivalent. Let's look at some of these protocols:

Bluetooth LE

Bluetooth Low Energy as the name suggests is a power efficient version of the standard Bluetooth protocol, specifically designed for devices where power consumption is a key requirement.

With Bluetooth LE supported on most of the new generation mobile platforms and operating systems, it provides an option for Bluetooth LE devices to connect to Bluetooth LE mobiles and devices instantly and connect to the cloud platform or interact with the mobile application. Products like health devices or smart watches can use Bluetooth LE and connect with a Smartphones to send data to the cloud for further analysis.

RFID

RFID protocol is used to communicate data between RFID tags and readers. RFID tags, described earlier in *Device Layer* section, are primarily used for tracking objects, while RFID readers reads the unique tag value which is then further processed by the system. A typical example of RFID in context of IoT is to track and trace assets or products, where products are tagged by RFID tags and device gateway is installed at entry and exit points which also act as a reader. .The data (possibly depicting movements of assets) is read by the reader and sent over to the cloud platform which can trigger warnings like an unauthorized movement of a particular asset.

NFC

Near Field Communication (NFC) is similar to RFID protocol with an exception that the NFC device can act as a tag as well as a reader. NFC is also used for peer to peer communication between devices, like NFC enabled Smartphone which can share data if the devices are near to each other.

NFC enabled phones can communicate with other NFC enabled devices and appliances like washing machine, microwave etc. by installing the required application on the phone which can help control the device or appliance remotely.

ZigBee / Z-wave

ZigBee and Z-wave protocols are used with devices having constrained environment like low processing power, memory and battery life. These protocols are typically used in home automation to create smart homes. They operate on low frequency radio networks. The frequency can be increased by forming a mesh network topology (connecting similar devices to form a mesh thereby extending communication range). ZigBee and Z-wave cannot directly connect to internet as they do not support IP networking. You would need a gateway device to route the data to internet.

Application protocols

Application protocols sit on top of TCP layer. They use TCP as a transport layer to communicate application specific messages. This section discusses some of the application protocols that can be used with embedded devices.

MQTT

MQ Telemetry Transport (MQTT) is a lightweight message oriented middleware (MOM) that is based on publish/subscribe model. The protocol is designed to be used for machine-to-machine communication that involves small data footprint. It works on the basis of hub/spoke topology. IoT devices are clients that connect to MQTT broker over the TCP protocol. The client devices subscribe to the messages published on a single or multiple topics. Topics itself can be structured hierarchically allowing to design an appropriate taxonomy specific to a particular domain, say home automation. MQTT broker supports multiple concurrent connections involving large number of devices. This protocol is widely used in resource constrained devices and networks where high bandwidth is an issue. Another variant is MQTT-SN that is designed to be used with sensor networks. It is applicable where data packet loss during transmission is not an issue. MQTT-SN works on a UDP transport.

CoAP

The Constrained Application Protocol (CoAP), as the name suggests it is a protocol used with resource constrained devices and networks. The protocol is design to be used with machine-to-machine communication applications. It is modelled on the concept of HTTP (request/response) but uses low data footprint. Unlike HTTP, CoAP runs over UDP transport with broadcast and multicast feature. The protocol is used in a client-server model, and supports REST style commands like GET, POST, PUT and DELETE. There also exists HTTP-CoAP mapping that can be leveraged to communicate to CoAP devices using HTTP protocol. CoAP also supports asynchronous model involving message communication.

AMQP

Advanced Message Queuing Protocol (AMQP) is another popular message oriented middleware that has slowly made its place in the world of IoT. The protocol supports both queue based and pub/sub messaging model. The messages can be processed in a transactional context. The AMQP protocol operates on TCP transport and ensures reliable message delivery. Apart from reliability, AMQP is also interoperable. Disparate client systems with different software languages can interoperate with AMQ servers. From the IoT perspective, sensor devices that generate loads of data are streamed to AMQ servers (either in a raw or processed form), which is then consumed by receivers to perform monitoring and analytics.

WebSocket

WebSocket protocol supports a persistent connection between a client and the server over a single TCP connection. WebSocket protocol is used to facilitate near real-time communication and data transfer from and to the server without the client/server polling for data updates and transmitting relevant updates without an explicit request between client and server. In context of IoT, WebSocket provides one of the alternative ways to provide real time communication between devices and Cloud applications as compared to protocols like MQTT and AMQP.

AllJoyn

AllJoyn is a collaborative open-source software framework that makes it easy for devices to discover, publish/broadcast itself and communicate with each other. AllJoyn was created to promote interoperability and seamless integration between devices and application through a set of core features. AllJoyn works across platforms that ranges from Android to iOS, Linux, OpenWRT Windows, OS X and embedded systems having limited memory and processing power capability.

Interoperability between devices and applications is the key to adoption and realization of a connected world and in future standards like AllJoyn would help bridge the interoperability gap.

Note - The AllSeen Alliance manages the AllJoyn open source project with software code using open standards to enable all the 'things' in the Internet of Things to work together. The initiative includes more than 170 member companies including leading consumer electronics manufacturers, home appliance makers, automotive companies, Internet of Things cloud providers, enterprise technology companies, innovative start-ups, chipset manufacturers, service providers, retailers and software developers.

DDS

DDS (Data Connectivity Standard) is part of OMG IoT standards, which enables network interoperability for connected machines, enterprise systems, and mobile device. DDS is a not a new protocol specification and was initially adopted for real-time communications. The DDS specification is available at http://portals.omg.org/dds/. DDS is used by many industries where real-time communication is required between systems. You can find the set of case studies at this link - http://portals.omg.org/dds/who-is-using-dds-2/

Industry Protocols

Industry protocols are designed to implement a connected solution specific to that industry. The protocols are proprietary in nature and enables industrial automation of some sorts. The section will describe some of the popular industry specific protocols.

BACnet

BACnet is a communication protocol used to create smart buildings. It enables building automation by providing infrastructure for applications to monitor and control network of BACnet devices. It facilitates exchange of information between building automation devices that aids in application management building functions. The communications between devices are handled in three areas: objects, services and transport. Objects represent information about the device. Services are actions initiated by devices. These services are classified in 5 categories: object access, device management, alarm and event, file transfer and virtual terminal. Transport represents the communication channel and the messaging protocol. BACnet supports seven transport layers that include the transport over Ethernet, ZigBee, Telephone line etc. The typical use case application would be to remotely monitor heat, lighting, ventilation, elevators and other aspects of building systems controlled by BACnet.

SCADA

Supervisory Control and Data Acquisition (SCADA) is a system that enables remote control and monitoring of industrial devices. SCADA solution is a network of systems that work together to provide industrial automation. A typical SCADA set up will have an industrial device like gas measurement sensors that will emit measurement signals and send it to specialized processing unit called as Remote Terminal Units (RTU) or Programmable Logic Controller (PLC). The processing unit reads the signal and processes it into digital format to be transmitted to Human Machine Interface (HMI) panels or control room workstations for the end user to control and monitor the industrial process flow. There is also a supervisory system that acts as a server and sits between PLCs and HMI workstations. There will be another workstation that will act as a communication gateway responsible for sending the data to the cloud or internet where it can be processed and analyzed using data processing platforms and visualization tools. SCADA network transport operates on a wide variety of communication media (both wired and wireless) that uses TCP and UDP protocols (like Modbus TCP) with cellular, radio or satellite networks. SCADA applications are widely used in industries like manufacturing, transportation, oil and gas, electric power, distribution and utilities, process industries, water and waste control, agriculture/irrigation etc.

Modbus

Modbus is a serial communication protocol widely used in industrial automation applications. It uses standard RS-485 and RS-232 serial port for communication. In a typical SCADA network, many sensors are connected to PLCs. The communication is achieved through the use of Modbus protocol. Popular Modbus protocols include Modbus RTU and Modbus TCP. Modbus RTU is a serial protocol conceptualized on the master/slave model. It is the most popular and widely used protocol in industries like building automation. Modbus TCP also known as Modbus Ethernet protocol is a modern approach towards industrial automation. It works exactly like Modbus RTU but with greater throughput. Modbus TCP can be used to connect industrial devices to the outside Internet world.

Core Platform Layer

The core platform layer provides a set of capabilities to connect, collect, monitor and control millions of devices. Let's look at each of the components of the core platform layer.

Protocol Gateway

An Enterprise IoT platform typically supports one protocol end to end like AMQP or MQTT as part of the overall stack. However in an IoT landscape, where there are no standardized protocols where all vendors can converge on, an Enterprise IoT stack needs to provide support for commonly used protocols, industry protocols, and support for evolving standards in future.

One option is to use a device gateway that we had discussed earlier to convert device proprietary protocols to the protocol supported by the platform for communication, but that may not always be possible as devices may connect directly or the device gateway may not support the protocol supported by the IoT stack. In order to support handling multiple protocols, a protocol gateway is used which does the conversion of the protocol supported by your IoT stack. Building an abstraction like protocol gateway would make it easier to support different protocols in future.

The protocol gateway layer provides connectivity to the devices over protocols supported by the IoT stack. Typically the communication is channelized to the messaging platform or middleware like MQTT or AMQP. The protocol gateway layer can also act as a facade for supporting different protocols, performing conversions across protocols and handing off the implementation to corresponding IoT messaging platform.

IoT Messaging Middleware

Messaging middleware is a software or an appliance that allows senders (publishers) and receivers (consumer's consuming the information) to distribute messages in a loosely coupled manner without physically connected to each other. A message middleware allows multiple consumers to receive messages from a single publisher or a single consumer can send messages to multiple senders.

Messaging middleware is not a new concept, it has been used as a backbone for message communication between enterprise systems, as an integration pattern with various distributed systems in a unified way or in-built as part of the application server.

In the context of IoT, the messaging middleware becomes a key capability providing a highly scalable, high performance middleware to accommodate vast number of ever growing connected devices. Gartner, Inc. forecasts that 4.9 billion connected things will be in use in 2015 and will reach 25 billion by 2020.

The IoT messaging middleware platform needs to provide various device management aspects like registering the devices, enabling storage of device meta-model, secure connectivity for devices, storage of device data for specified interval and dashboards to view connected devices. The storage requirements imposed by an IoT platform is quite different from a traditional messaging platform as we are looking at terabytes of data from the connected devices and at the same time ensuring high performance and fault tolerance guarantees. The IoT messaging middleware platform typically hold the device data for the specified interval and in-turn a dedicated storage service is used to scale, compute and analyze information.

The device meta-model that we mentioned earlier is one of the key aspects for an Enterprise IoT application. A device meta-model can be visualized as a set of metadata about the device, parameters (input and output) and functions (send, receive) that a device may emit or consume. By designing the device meta-model as part of the IoT solution, you could create a generalized solution for each industry/verticals which abstracts out the dependency between data send by the devices and data used by the IoT platform and services that works on that data. You can even work on a virtual device using the device model and build and test the entire application, without physically connected the device. We would talk about the device meta-model in detail in the solution section.

All the capabilities of the IoT stack, starting from the messaging platform right up to the cognitive platform are typically made available as services over the cloud platform which can be readily consumed to build IoT applications.

We would revisit the topic in detail in Chapter 3, when we talk about the IoT capabilities offered by popular cloud vendors and using open source software.

Data Storage
The data storage component deals with storage of continuous stream of data from devices. As mentioned earlier we are looking at a highly scalable storage service which can storage terabytes of data and enable faster retrieval of data. The data needs to be replicated across servers to ensure high availability and no single point of failure.

Typically a NoSQL database or high performance optimized storage is used for storing data. The design of data model and schema becomes a key to enable faster retrieval, perform computations and makes it easier for down processing systems which uses the data for analysis. For instance, if you are storing data from a connected car every minute, your data can be broken down in ids and values , the id field would not change for a connected car instance but values would keep on changing – for instance like speed =60 km/hour, speed =65 km/hour etc. In that case instead of storing key=value, you can store key=value1, value2 … and key=timeint1, timeint2 and so on. The data represents a sequence of values for a specific attribute over a period of time. This concept is referred to as time series and database which supports these requirements is called as Time Series database. You could use NoSQL databases like MongoDB or Cassandra and design your schema in a way that it is optimized for storing time series data and doing statistical computations. Not all use cases may require the use of time series database, buts is an important concept to keep in mind while designing IoT applications.

In the context of an enterprise IoT application, the data storage layer should also support storage and handling of unstructured and semi structured information. The data from these sources (structured, unstructured and semi structured) can be used to correlate and derive insights. For instance, information data from equipment manual (unstructured text of information) can be fed into the system and sensor data from the connected equipment can be correlated with the equipment manuals for raising critical functional alerts and suggesting corrective measures.

The IoT messaging middleware service usually provides a set of configurations to store the incoming data from the devices automatically into the specified storage service.

In Chapter 3, we would talk about various storage service options provided by cloud providers for storing a massive amount of data from connected devices.

Data aggregation and filter

The IoT core platform deals with raw data coming from multiple devices and not all data needs to be consumed and treated equally by your application. We talked about device gateway pattern earlier which can filter data before sending it over to the cloud platform. Your device gateway may not have the luxury and computation power to store and filter out volumes of data or be able to filter out all scenarios. In some solutions, the devices can directly connect to the platform without a device gateway. As part of your IoT application, you need to design this carefully as what data needs to be consumed and what data might not be relevant in that context. The data filter component could provide simple rules to complex conditions based on your data dependency graph to filter out the incoming data. The data mapper component is also used to convert raw data from the devices into an abstract data model which is used by rest of the components.

In some cases, you need to contextualize the device data with more information, like aggregating the current data from devices with existing asset management software to retrieve warranty information of physical devices or from a weather station for further analysis. That's where the data aggregation components comes in which allows to aggregate and enrich the incoming data. The aggregation component can also be part of the messaging stream processing framework that we will discuss in the next section, but instead of using complex flows for just aggregating information, this requirement could be easily handled without much overhead using simplified flows and custom coding, without using a stream processing infrastructure.

Analytics Platform Layer

The Analytics platform layer provides a set of key capabilities to analyze large volumes of information, derive insights and enable applications to take required action.

Stream Processing

Real-time stream processing is about processing streams of data from devices (or any source) in real-time, analyze the information, do computations and trigger events for required actions. The stream processing infrastructure directly interacts with the IoT Messaging Middleware component by listening to specified topics. The stream processing infrastructure acts as a subscriber, which consumes messages (data from devices) arriving continuously at the IoT Messaging Middleware layer.

A typical requirement for stream processing software includes high scalability, handling a large volume of continuous data, provide fault tolerance and support for interactive queries in some form like using SQL queries which can act on the stream of data and trigger alerts if conditions are not met.

Most of the big data implementations started with Hadoop which supported only batch processing, but with the advent of various real-time streaming technologies and changing the requirement of dealing with massive amount of data in real-time, applications are now migrating to stream based technology that can handle data processing in real-time. Stream processing platform like Apache Spark Streaming enables you to write stream jobs to process streaming data using Spark API. It enables you to combine streams with batch and interactive queries. Projects already using existing Hadoop based batch processing system can still take the benefit of real-time stream processing by combining the batch processing queries with stream based interactive queries offered by Spark Streaming.

The stream processing engine acts as a data processing backbone which can hand off streams of data to multiple other services simultaneously for parallel execution or to your own custom application to process the data. For instance, a stream processing instance can invoke a set of custom applications, one which can execute complex rules and other invoking a machine learning service.

We would talk about the concepts and implementation in detail in Chapter 3.

Machine Learning

Following is the Wikipedia definition of Machine Learning –

"Machine learning explores the study and construction of algorithms that can learn from and make predictions on data"

In simple terms, machine learning is how we make computers learn from data using various algorithms without explicitly programming it, so it can provide the required outcome – like classifying an email as spam or not spam or predicting a real estate price based on historical values and other environmental factors.

Machine learning types are typically classified into 3 broad categories

- Supervised learning – In this methodology we provide labeled data (input and desired output) and train the system to learn from it and predict outcomes. Classic example of supervised learning is your Facebook application automatically recognizing your friend's photo based on your earlier tags or your email application recognizing spam automatically.
- Unsupervised learning – In this methodology, we don't provide labeled data and leave it to algorithms to find hidden structure in unlabelled data. For instance, clustering similar news in one bucket or market segmentation of users are examples of unsupervised learning.
- Reinforcement learning – Reinforcement learning is about systems learning by interacting with the environment rather than being taught. For instance, a computer playing chess knows what it means to win or lose, but how to move forward in the game to win is learned over a period of time through interactions with the user.

Machine learning process typically consists of 4 phases as shown in the figure below – understanding the problem definition and the expected business outcome, data cleansing and analysis, model creation, training and evaluation. This is an iterative process where models are continuously

refined to improve its accuracy. We would cover the steps in detail in
Chapter 3.

From an IoT perspective, machine learning models are developed based
on different industry vertical use cases. Some can be common across the
stack like anomaly detection and some use case specific, like condition
based maintenance and predictive maintenance for manufacturing
related use cases.

In Chapter 2 and 3, we will further revisit machine learning concepts and
usages in detail based on real world use cases.

Actionable Insights (Events & Reporting)

Actionable Insights, as part of Analytics Platform layer, are set of services
that make it easier for invoking the required action based on the analyzed
data. The action can trigger events; call external services or update
reports and dashboards in real-time. For example, invoking a third party
service using a HTTP/REST connector for creating a work flow order based
on the outcome of the condition based maintenance service or invoking a
single API for mobile push notification across mobile devices to notify
maintenance events. Actionable insights can also be configured from real-
time dashboards that enable you to create rules and actions that need to
be triggered.

The service should also allow your application custom code to be
executed to carry out desired functionality. Your custom code can be
uploaded in the cloud or built using the runtimes provided and integrate
with rest of the stack through the platform APIs.

Cognitive Platform Layer

Let's first understand what is cognitive computing. Cognitive computing are systems that are designed to make computers think and learn like human brain. Similar to an evolution of a human mind from a new born to teenager to an adult, where new information is learned and existing information augmented, cognitive system learn through the vast amount of information fed to it. Such a system is trained on a set of information or data, so that it can understand the context and help in making informed decisions.

For example, if you look at any learning methodology, a human mind learns and understands the context. It is able to answer questions based on learning's and also make informed judgement based on prior experiences. Similarly cognitive systems are modelled to learn from past set of reference data set (or learning's) and enable users to make informed decisions. Cognitive systems can be thought of non-programming systems which learn through the set of information, training, interactions and a reference data set.

Cognitive systems in the context of IoT would play a key role in future. Imagine 10 years down the line where every piece of system is connected to the internet and probably an integral part of everyday lives and information being shared continuously, how you would like to interact with these smart devices which surround you. It would be virtually talking to smart devices and devices responding to you based on your action and behaviour.

A good example can be of a connected car. As soon as you enter the car it should recognize you automatically, adjust your car seats, start the car and start reading your priority emails. This is not programmed but learned over time. The car over a period of time should also provide recommendations on how to improve the mileage based on your driving patterns.

In future, you should be able to speak to devices through tweets, spoken words, gestures and devices would be able to understand the context and respond accordingly. For instance, a smart device as part of connected home would react differently as compared to devices in a connected car.

For a connected home, a cognitive IoT system can learn from you, set things up for you based on your patterns and movements, be it waking you up at the right time, start your coffee vending machines, sending you a WhatsApp message to start washing machine if you missed to start it based on your routine or take care of the home lighting system based on your family preferences. Imagine putting a smart controller and set of devices around your home, which observes you over a period of time and start making intelligent decisions on Day 10 and continuously learn from you and your family interactions.

From an implementation perspective, at a very high level, building a cognitive platform requires a combination of various technologies like machine learning, natural language processing, reinforcement learning, domain adoption through various techniques and algorithms apart from the IoT stack capabilities that we have discussed earlier. The cognitive platform layer should enable us to analyze structured, semi-structured and unstructured information, perform correlations, and derive insights.

This is one of the areas where we would see a lot of innovation and investment happening in future and would be a key differentiator for connected products and extension to one's digital lives.

Solutions Layer
This section will discuss industrial or consumer applications built on top of the IoT stack leveraging the various services (messaging, streaming, machine learning etc.) offered by the IoT stack.

Solutions can be broken down into 2 parts – Solution Templates and Applications. Following diagram shows the concept of Solution Templates and Applications.

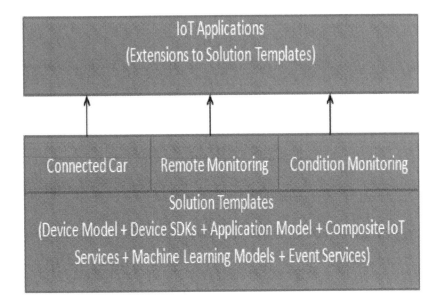

Solution Templates are common set of services which are developed for specific or generalized use case that provides a head start to build IoT applications and are extended to build custom IoT applications. Building an IoT application requires a common set of tasks and services, configurations of components via dashboard or APIs and the entire process can be simplified and abstracted through the use of solution templates. The key component of a solution template is the abstract data model.

The solution's abstract data model is a combination of device data model that we discussed earlier in IoT Messaging Middleware section plus your application data model specific to that domain/industry/vertical use case. The services from the solution template uses the abstract data model for communication, instead of directly dealing with data from sensors. The abstract data model is different for different industries. A connected car abstract data model would be different from connected-home, but if the abstract data model is properly envisioned and designed, it can provide the much needed abstraction between devices and platforms.

As an example, for a connected car solution, the abstract data model could be a vehicle's runtime data + GPS data + asset data of the vehicle, which constitutes the device meta-model and the application data model. The abstract data model then can be used for various other connected car use cases. It is more like creating a template that can be applied on different connected solutions within the same domain or industry. For example, a connected vehicle solution for sedan may be different for an SUV. But a common abstract data model, to some extent gives the basic connected car functionality applicable to all connected cars irrespective of model or make. Some examples of solution templates could be remote monitoring, predictive maintenance or geospatial analysis.

One can use solution templates to build application based on customer requirements. Please note a predictive maintenance requirement would be different for each industries, the devices and equipment across manufacturing plants that needs to be connected would be different, data from devices would be totally different, the historical data would be different and lot of effort would be required to just connect and integrate the manufacturing equipment to the platform.

However the steps required building a predictive maintenance system should be pretty much the same. For instance, it would require working with existing asset management solutions to identify master data for equipment, connect to multiple data sources to extract, cleanse normalize, aggregate the data (for instance the data from historical database) and convert it to a form which can be consumed by services (the abstract model) and develop machine learning models which uses the abstract model to predict outcomes. All these common steps and services can be abstracted into a solution template and application provider can use this template for providing implementations or integrations based on the requirements.

Let's take another example, a manufacturing company already knows what parameters are required for servicing an equipment, what information needs to be monitored, what is remaining lifecycle of the machinery (not on actual, but based on when it was bought) and what are the external factors (temperature, weather, etc.) which can cause a machine to possibly fail. This information can be easily turned into an abstract data model. Machine learning models can be developed and executed which uses this abstract data model to predict machinery failures. The only task remaining would be to map the data from the sensors to the abstract model. The abstract data model provides a generic abstraction of the data dependency between devices and the IoT platform.

However, existing platform and solutions in the market is far from the concept of building solutions templates which builds on the abstract data model due to multiple factors – heterogeneity of devices, domain expertise and integration challenges. In future, not just the platform, but the solution templates and applications being offered would be a key differentiator between various IoT cloud offerings. An IoT cloud provider would enter into partnership with manufacturing unit and system integrators to build viable, generic and reusable solutions.

IoT Security and Management

Building and deploying an end-to-end enterprise IoT application is a complex process. There are multiple players involved (hardware providers, embedded device manufacturers, network providers, platform providers, solution providers, system integrators) which increase the complexity of integration, security and management. In order to address the complexity holistically, an enterprise IoT stack needs to provide a set of capabilities which would ease the overall process and take care of end to end cross cutting concerns like security and performance. In this section we will talk about key aspects at minimum which should be addressed by an enterprise IoT stack.

Device Management

Device management includes aspects like device registration, secure device provisioning and access from device to cloud platform and cloud platform to device, monitoring and administration, troubleshooting and pushing firmware and software updates to devices including gateway devices. A device gateway might also include local data storage and data filter component as discussed earlier which needs to be updated in case of new versions or support patches.

An enterprise IoT platform should provide administration console and/or APIs to allow devices to register on the platform securely. The device registration capability should allow fine grained access and permissions on what operations the device can carry out in the context of that application. Some devices may require only one way communication from cloud to device for handling firmware updates and some others would need a bidirectional communication like gateways. Some devices may only have read access while some device can post messages to the platform. The security aspects should provide configuration related security as well as security over the specified protocol. For instance, even if an intruder get access to the devices, the intruder may not be able to post the messages to the platform. Device SDKs should provide libraries that are safer to access thereby ensuring that there is no vulnerability in the communication process.

Monitoring and administration

Monitoring and administration is about managing the lifecycle of the device. The lifecycle operations include register, start, pause, stop activities and the ability to trigger events/commands to and from devices. A pause state could be a valid requirement in use cases like a health tracking devices as opposed to a connected car. The ability to add custom states based on the requirements should be a part of the monitoring and administration capabilities. Monitoring should also capture various parameters to help troubleshoot devices like device make, software installed, library installed, last connected date, last data sent, storage available, current status etc. For instance, a device gateway may have stopped functioning due to it running out of storage space. This could happen if the remote synchronization service was not running to transfer out the storage data from the device and clear the space. Monitoring can also identify suspicious activity, and therefore needs a mechanism to address it.

Lastly the device management should provide capabilities to update firmware, software and dependent libraries on the devices securely through administrative commands or through auto-update features. Deploying device updates across millions of devices still needs to be solved at large. In next section, we would talk about various deployment options.

Deployment

Deployment of IoT applications needs to be looked at holistically, right from IoT devices, networks and topology, cloud services and end solutions and taking care of end to end security. We are already seeing lot of partnership in this space, where device manufacturers are partnering with cloud providers that enables devices to register with the cloud provider in a secured way.

This is an area which needs lot of attention and innovations and we feel the next investments would happen in this space. This would include providing an end to end set of tools and environment to design and simulate connected products, deployment and management of millions of devices, using docker images for device updates, testing network topologies to services and solutions which build up the IoT application.

Summary

In this chapter we went through the key concepts on Internet of Things and described the Enterprise IoT stack in detail. An Enterprise IoT stack provides a host of capabilities that makes it easier to build IoT applications. We went though each of the components in details and talked about the functionality and how these components interact with each other.

Chapter 2. Application of IoT

In this chapter, we will look at the application of IoT taking examples of different industry domains.

We will take an example of industrial manufacturing domain where automation and some instrumentation already exist and they need to incrementally move towards a connected solution. We will also look at the application of IoT in the automotive and home industry by demonstrating the use cases of connected vehicle and connected home respectively. The concepts mentioned in this chapter can be applied to realize any IoT solution.

Manufacturing

Large manufacturers have been using some automation and smart technology to streamline and optimize their processes and improve their operation and production efficiency. However, as manufacturers start moving towards the next industrial revolution (Industry 4.0 or Industrial Internet of Things(IIoT)) and technologies available today that can analyze massive volume, variety, and velocity of data generated by various machines and sensors, there arises an opportunity to streamline this information to further improve the manufacturing process and most importantly start designing and developing connected products that can enhance customer satisfaction and services and open up avenues for new financial business models.

Note – The term Industry 4.0 and Industrial Internet of Things are usually used interchangeably, but they have different context and reference. Industry 4.0 is a term coined by German government, it's marks the fourth industrial revolution and can be described as the digitalization of industrial sector, especially for manufacturing. Industrial Internet of Things is about enabling and applying IoT across industries. Also check out Industrial Internet Consortium (http://www.industrialinternetconsortium.org/) a non profit organization, founded by AT&T, Cisco, GE, IBM and Intel to collaborate and set the

Let's take an example of a leading elevator manufacturing company which supplies elevators across the globe. The elevators already have some instrumentation built in, like door sensor, a weight sensor which triggers an alert like beep in case of overload etc. but the elevator company has no visibility on how the elevators are being used across the globe and therefore, raises the following important questions:

Are these elevators working as expected and utilized as per the specification?

Is there a failure condition?

What kind of failure has occurred?

How are failures to be handled?

What is the typical acceptable downtime?

Which agency is handling the failure condition?

How effective is the after-sales service in that region?

Is there a competent expertise available to handle a given failure condition?

Are the spare parts available to quickly start the restoration process?

Proper application of IoT can address the above questions by designing a connected solution that will help capture and analyze the product usage, operational and failure data and ultimately improve the customer satisfaction and services.

IoT can not only transform the end products but the entire manufacturing process right from the start where the elevators are manufactured. The supply chain process and logistics can also be streamlined to enhance operational efficiency and productivity and deliver better financial gains.

IoT is an incremental journey, it's an evolution and any manufacturing IoT realization can be broken down into the following five phases:

- Monitoring & Utilization
- Condition based maintenance
- Predictive Maintenance
- Optimization
- Connecting 'connected solutions'

IoT in Manufacturing

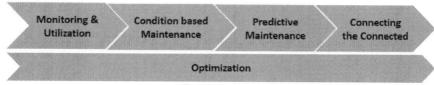

Lifecycle Phases

Monitoring & Utilization

Monitoring and utilization are the first steps of an IoT journey. This is an umbrella phase which itself consists of many requirements.

For the large scale manufacturer, to enable seamless monitoring and utilization of their systems, the step usually comprises of:

1. Asset Management
   - Identifying assets that need to be monitored

2. Instrumentation
   - Leveraging existing instrumentation investments (if any)
   - Adding new hardware capability (new sensors/actuators/microcontrollers) based on the design and requirements of the connected solution.

3. Handle Connectivity
   - Adding connectivity to devices as per above points (1) and (2). We would talk about various patterns, the device directly connected to the core platform; intercommunication between devices or a device gateway connected to the core platform which communicates with existing devices using a low level or existing proprietary protocols.

4. Perform Monitoring

Asset Management

To start with you need to identify the set of physical assets that needs to be monitored. For example, for an elevator manufacturing company an elevator is an asset, which contains various sub-assets like doors, input control buttons (open, close, call, alarm etc.), elevator telephone etc. Similarly, for a connected car manufacturer, the car is an asset which contains various sub assets like engine, brakes, tires etc. and for any manufacturing plant, machinery equipment, conveyor systems etc. are examples of assets that needs to be monitored. An asset contains a set of metadata, for example, a car engine can have a manufacturer's name, capacity, year of manufacturing etc. Asset management is perceived through asset metadata and its dependencies with other assets. Manufacturers typically have a software platform or an application to manage the lifecycle of its assets. While moving towards implementing IoT, the existing asset management design or application may not be sufficient or good enough for building next generation connected solution. Right from requirements, design to simulation, creating connected products and its lifecycle management, will require a completely new approach and a set of next generation software products to realize a connected solution. We envision a set of new emerging software products to tackle requirements for designing connected solution. For instance, understanding a dependency between a car engine, engine oil, led indicators and brakes through the system's metadata and making use of analytics platform to perform analysis on the actual sensor data in a connected car solution, could help derive correlations easily and suggest measures to tackle failure condition. The design of connected products is a separate topic in itself and outside the scope of this book.

Instrumentation

In a manufacturing world, some kind of instrumentation is already employed, like the use case of the elevator which we talked about earlier. The elevators already have built-in sensors, but these sensors are not connected to any platform, (the platform here maps to core platform in our architecture diagram - Refer Chapter 1) so as to enable transfer and analysis of the data. Moreover the protocol and connectivity (maps to communication layer in our architecture diagram-- Refer Chapter 1) for the various hardware components (or devices) in the elevator and their interactions would be very proprietary in nature.

Based on the requirements of the connected product, new hardware components (devices, microcontroller, sensors etc.) might also be required. For instance, in a connected elevator design, the elevators now have new requirements to maintain an optimum temperature for smooth functioning, taking into account surrounding external factors (external factors may vary in different regions). Now the new design could also break down an operating ambient temperature into multiple levels of degradations, monitor this remotely or via notification and use this information to schedule services. For instance, take the following example where X is the optimum temperature that needs to be maintained and if X is greater than Threshold value, the degradations process starts. Lastly, if no action is taken from start of degradation beyond Y days, a critical failure alert message is sent to the elevator company.

X being optimum temperature,

X > Threshold Value -> Needs attention within 5 days. Elevator is still functional but with limited load. The load is cut down from 300 kg to 150 kg.

At this stage, details about the suggestive spare part changes, location of the spare part, suggested service vendor nearest to current location is also made available by the system. It's easier for system to detect the GPS coordinates of the connected system, look at the inventory and service vendors based on the region and schedule maintenance services. At this stage, elevator is operational but with reduced load and have controlled movement of people using the elevator.

X > Threshold Value (Date) – Y Days –> Critical Failure alert. This is final alert to repair the defective part, along with a good time to repair the elevator based on people movement during that week and projections to ensure minimum downtime and least impact to passengers. The above is only one such example. A manufacturer could employ many such requirements, which would require design changes right from microcontrollers to adding new hardware components. Again, this is an incremental effort, one can take gradual steps by identifying and adding new hardware component and then connecting along the way to the core platform for data transmission. The data is then used to correlate and perform analysis at the core platform layer to understand failure conditions and patterns.

Handle Connectivity

There are 3 general connectivity patterns which allows devices to communicate to the core platform

- Connecting device directly to core platform
- Connecting devices to an intelligent system and/or device gateway.
- Inter communication with devices.

Based on the use cases, the connectivity option would differ. If there is a requirement to process the data locally and take action and/or a requirement to map different proprietary protocols to a standardized protocol, a device gateway is generally used which will translate the incoming protocol instructions to that of the target platform. The requirement also depends on the power consumption capacity of the device and it may not make sense for all devices to directly connect to the core platform.

For the elevator manufacturing use case, the devices (doors, motor temperature, shaft alignment etc.) is already instrumented and connected to a central device (microcontroller). The central device can be IoT enabled or a new device gateway can be installed which talks to the central device. It can be done by installing the required platform libraries and code which connects to the core platform, understands and map the data from controller into a payload object (like JSON) and submits the payload to the core platform.

Libraries are available which supports making a device IoT enabled, like the Eclipse based Paho library (http://www.eclipse.org/paho/) which is an open-source client implementation of MQTT that can be installed on devices supporting C, Java, Android, Python, C++, JavaScript and .NET programming model. This is of course with the assumption that the core platform supports the MQTT protocol.

The choice of library depends on the device being IoT enabled, the programming language supported by the device (C, C++, JavaScript, etc.), the protocols supported by the core platform (MQTT, AMQP, REST etc.) and the client library available for the device. One can also use REST style invocations to connect to core platform. Core platform can provide SDKs for various devices that provide APIs to convert the device data into required payload supported by the core platform. For example, open source projects like Connect-The-Dots (https://github.com/Azure/connectthedots) allow devices to connect to Microsoft IoT services.

Not all data from the IoT enabled device, need to be transferred to the core platform. The IoT enabled device gateway can employ local storage to filter out the data (like start and stop activity for each floor in case of elevators) and transfer only relevant data to the platform. We don't want to clog the network and the platform with data that is not relevant and at the same time make sure enough data is transmitted from the systems to analyze important indicators, operational activities of various sensors, identify failures and use the historical events and data for future prediction of machines. Identifying and understanding the critical aspect of the data and prioritizing the same should be a key decision factor for building IoT applications.

Edge gateways can also be used which is geographically located closer to the devices or the device gateways, which can normalize the data before moving it to the core platform. For instance, to a global connected car manufacturer, it would make sense to have edge gateways at respective locations which can then streamline data movement to the core platform. We would see lot of such patterns evolving in future that would enable scalability and connectivity of billion of devices.

As new production ready devices are manufactured for IoT, we envision the required firmware and connectivity code would be part of the device design and shipped with some standardized protocol support. In an ideal world, we should have converged on one standardized protocol for IoT (like the AllJoyn protocol which is gaining momentum) to make connectivity seamless, but in reality many such standardized protocol would exist and there would be an integration approach required to make them work seamlessly.

Another example is of water and waste water manufacturing plant which uses SCADA network to gather, monitor and process data. The manufacturing plant already employs sensors and proprietary protocols that monitor temperature, relative humidity, pH, barometric pressure, and various other environmental parameters. To be agile and scalable, traditional manufacturing systems need to adopt technologies to store and aggregate volumes of data from sensors, monitor systems in real-time, analyze the data and give out insights which were not possible earlier and eventually create predictive models to predict equipment failure or a possible outcome.

This is especially true for manufacturing companies which might have already employed a wide variety of protocols. The ideal approach or pattern would be to install an intelligent system of gateways to convert these protocols and make them communicate securely with the core platform. Manufacturers can incrementally move their legacy devices into the realm of IoT ecosystem by connecting them to the outside world through intelligent gateways. For instance, BACnet is the widely used protocol for smart building and products like Microsoft AllJoyn Device System Bridge, allows existing devices that uses BACnet to connect to an AllJoyn network, thereby enabling existing devices to connect with IoT core platform and also with new AllJoyn devices.

In future, we would see the connected product design being a key requirement as part of the manufacturing process.

Perform Monitoring

Once the devices are connected and data from the devices is made available to the core platform, the monitoring part kicks in. The device data is usually stored in a database (possibly a time series database) for further analysis and predictions and at the same time can be acted upon by the system for real-time analysis. The monitoring phase typically involves providing a dashboard to track the devices remotely across the globe and how each device is being utilized as per the specification. The specifications are available as part of the metadata we talked about it earlier in Asset Management section.

For instance, in case of the r elevator use case, the optimum motor temperature should be not be more than 40 degree Celsius or the air condition temperature inside the elevator should be at least 18 degree Celsius at peak load.

Monitoring can also be used to detect if the elevators are installed and functioning as per the specification. For instance, every manufacturer provides a checklist for regular maintenance activity that can be tracked through remote monitoring. Following is a sample checklist which is provided by City of Chicago – Department of Buildings for compliance purpose. As you see most of the test requirements can be handled by adding sensors and monitoring it remotely.

DEPARTMENT OF BUILDINGS

Periodic Tests of Electric Elevators - Report Form

Test Performed: Category 1 ☐   Category 5 ☐

Building & Unit Information

Building Name	Owner/Building Management Name
Building Address	Unit Identification / Unit PIN

Category 1 Test Requirement	ASME Section	Pass	Fail	N/A
Oil Buffers	8.11.2.2.1			
Safeties	8.11.2.2.2			
Governors	8.11.2.2.3			
Slack-Rope Devices on Winding Drum Machines	8.11.2.2.4			
Normal and Final Terminal Stopping Devices	8.11.2.2.5			
Firefighters' Emergency Operation	8.11.2.2.6			
Standby or Emergency Power Operation	8.11.2.2.7			
Power Operation of Door System	8.11.2.2.8			
Broken Rope, Tape, or Chain Switch	8.11.2.2.9			
E/E/PES Electrical Protective Devices	8.11.2.2.10			

Category 5 Test Requirement	ASME Section	Pass	Fail	N/A
Car and Counterweight Safeties	8.11.2.3.1			
Governors	8.11.2.3.2			
Oil Buffers	8.11.2.3.3			
Braking System.	8.11.2.3.4			
Emergency and Standby Power Operation	8.11.2.3.5			
Emergency Terminal Stopping and Speed Limiting Devices	8.11.2.3.6			

In the future, environmental requirements like energy efficiency, passenger safety and control compliance can be met through the remote monitoring and used for auditing and inspection eventually.

As the manufacturers start embracing IoT with the concept of connected products in mind, we would see a new class of products in future that will change the complete dynamics of manufacturing process. Imagine a self-test on the elevator which automatically evaluates the compliance parameters and publishes a report as part of the audit and quality procedures in a connected environment. (In short, an elevator would be compliant and secured 24 * 7).

Once the systems and devices are being monitored, next step is to use the information to provide timely maintenance of the assets based on the specification and its operating condition. We refer it as condition based maintenance.

Condition based maintenance

Condition based Maintenance (CBM) is about using the actual data gathered from the devices to decide what maintenance activity needs to be performed on the physical assets being monitored.

The connected device provides a set of continuous measurements (temperature, vibrations, air pressure, heat etc.) for the physical asset. This data along with the required operating specification of the physical assets can be used to create rules for maintenance activities and taking corrective action.

For the elevator use case, we talked about operating temperature requirement earlier as part of the instrumentation design. With the device data being available, the maintenance service can be scheduled whenever the degradation of asset starts.

For example,

X being optimum temperature,

X > Threshold Value –> Alert the service professional. The service professional can inspect the elevator remotely and approve the spare part suggested by the system. The elevators can continue to be functional under limited load and the load sensor rule now triggers at 150 kg instead of 300 kg. This ensures at any given point load does not increases beyond the expected value in case of degradation.

Take another example of a scheduled maintenance service for your automobile. The service schedule is usually specified as part of the manufacturer's operation manual based on the average operating condition rather than the actual usage and condition of the automobile. Using condition based maintenance, the service and maintenance activity, like the oil change in your vehicle should be triggered when the service and replacement is needed based on actual, rather than a predetermined schedule.

There are two approaches to arrive at condition based maintenance:

First approach is by creating predetermined rules based on actual value provided by the devices and executing the required action. For example, if optimum temperature of an elevator is > 40 and load > 150 kg, execute load alert/beep rule and start the elevator only when load falls below 150 kg.

The rule can be a simple rule or a combination of rules. The rules can be visually modelled using a programming language or a tool supported by the core platform. The rules are created using the parameters or fields of the device payload. In the above example, optimum temperature, elevator load are the fields defined as part of the payload.

The second approach is monitoring the values and detecting anomaly. The anomaly detection is about identifying the data and events which doesn't conform to the expected pattern as compared to other items in the data set. For example, assume you haven't defined any rules for optimum temperature functionality and data from the devices is being collected every second, say 15, 15, 17, 18 and on the third day you see this pattern 29,.30, 30, 29..., clearly the values read on the first day are less than half of the values read on the third day. This signifies an anomaly in the system, which can trigger an alert for someone to inspect the system. Another example would be in case of fire, where this might be detected as an anomaly by the system indicating the dramatic rise in the temperature. There could be another case where fire sensors itself could be tracking fire events. These two cases could be combined to derive a correlation and thereby enabling you to make a more precise observation.

All anomalies might not necessarily be real problems, but detecting anomaly should be a key requirement to ensure any susceptive exceptions are being caught by the system.

Tip - Anomalies can be detected using unsupervised machine learning algorithms like K-means. Libraries such as Spark MLlib provide first class support for many machine learning algorithms.

In future, we could see pre-built templates available for industry verticals which provide the domain model, rules, process flows, machine learning models, anomaly detectors and the job of the system integrator would be to map the device data into the domain model, extend the data model and customize the flow based on the client requirements.

There may be hundreds or thousands of such rules in a complex manufacturing system and it becomes very imperative to capture such requirements as part of your connected design. The connected design phase is yet to catch on and most of the noise is around IoT platforms and implementations. The futuristic software products will provide an end to end IoT implementations from a connected design perspective and also provide large scale simulations to simulate the design and the end product.

Predictive Maintenance

Predictive maintenance is the ability of the system to predict a machine failure. Predictive maintenance phase comprises of 2 parts - one is the ability to predict when the machine/asset failure would happen and secondly to perform maintenance activity before the malfunction happens. Predictive maintenance is one of the most widely discussed topics in the IoT ecosystem.

The first two phases of the manufacturing IoT involved monitoring and condition based maintenance. These phases can provide us with enough historical data, learning's, correlation between the data, type of failures and corrective action taken and enable to predict possible failures and what actions needs to be performed on the concerned asset.

In many places, you would read that predictive maintenance is same or a part of condition-based maintenance. We chose to call it out separately as the scope and implementations are quite different. Both deals with ensuring the maintenance are carried out before failure. The condition based maintenance primarily use monitoring, rules, and anomaly detection techniques; while predictive maintenance takes a step further to analyze volumes of historical or trend data, correlations, and machine specifications to predict an outcome. Predicting an outcome is very complex and an ongoing task, which requires to be handled separately.

A simple use case is using the information of the assets and its lifecycle and actual 'wear and tear' data of the parts provided through the connected devices, one can possibly predict the remaining life cycle of an asset and when should the maintenance be required. Imagine a dashboard, which lists the assets and its metadata, like manufacturing date, installed date, type etc. along with its actual usage and maintenance activity carried out during condition based maintenance phase. It also depicts external factors and predictions on remaining life cycle of the asset and a maintenance date. These factors can be used to plan a minimum maintenance downtime, schedule spare parts delivery and ensure maintenance is executed with least impact.

Secondly every manufacturer typically has historical maintenance records of the systems and usage data in some form, which needs to be converted into required format and can be a valuable input to predict the maintenance activity.

Going back to the elevator use case, take the example of the elevator lift cables. Can a system predict when the elevator lift cables need to be changed? Manufacturing innovations are happening in elevator cables, like using super light carbon fibre ropes that increase the lifespan of the cables, but still changing the lift cables is a costly maintenance activity and at the same time its failure can have a considerable downtime. Ensuring availability of new lift cables, specialized technicians availability, compliance check and all these factors can impact the business operations considerably.

In order to carry out any predictive maintenance for elevator lift cables, the manufacturer needs to look at what data points would be required to predict the failure. As part of its connect product design, the manufacturer had probably installed a sensor to track the running time or distance served by the cable, a sensor to detect if the elevator is descending faster than its designated speed and start and stop instances of the elevator. Sensor input together with the cable's specified life expectancy can be used to predict when the lift cables need to be replaced. In an actual scenario, many more such data sets need to be provided to predict outcomes.

Predictive maintenance involves building out machine learning models based on volumes of data. Developing machine learning models require considerable time and effort. It's virtually impossible to expect a system to devise a predictive model which is always 100% accurate (not even human operate with that level of accuracy :)), but should be considerable enough to suggest a cause of possible failure with reasonable accuracy.

Open source scalable machine learning models like Spark MLlib or commercial offerings like SPSS from IBM or Azure ML for Microsoft can aid in building predictive models. The real challenge is building feature sets (attributes) and using algorithms like Support Vector Machines, Logistic Regression, and Decision Trees or an ensemble model using multiple machine learning algorithms to predict an outcome.

The model once developed can be integrated into your IoT platform (as part of the Analytics Platform layer –refer Chapter 1) to predict outcomes in real-time. We would talk about this in detail in our next chapter as part of the services offered by various IoT platforms.

In future, we should see specialized pre-shipped predictive maintenance services targeted for various industries/verticals like connected car, elevator maintenance, wind turbines etc. These services would provide a generalized machine learning model developed using various factors we talked about earlier. System Integrators would play a key role in building the new machine learning model or use existing machine learning models and integrate with the IoT platform. For instance, take an example of a connected car, using the OBD device (actual diagnostic data at runtime) + GPS location, along with asset metadata (like type and make of car, manufacturing date of various parts and its specifications), a generalized machine learning model can be developed which can help predict maintenance activities and failures for any car type. This assumes that you should be able to look up the metadata for the car and its specifications, for instance the AUDI car type model maintenance service requirements would be different as compared to BMW or an AUDI of different model. The generalized data model (a connected car would have different input/output parameters as compared to a connected elevator) used by the machine learning model would also be a key component to help build predictive models effectively.

Many manufacturers are taking step in this direction but building predictive models with good amount of accuracy is not an easy task and this space would see lot of competition, partnership and innovations from manufacturers to software platform provider to system integrators.

Optimization

Optimization phase is all about identifying new insights based on the existing data that can further help refine the manufacturing process. Large volume of data generated by the devices, together with events generated by the system and various insights from predictive and condition based maintenance opens up the door for identifying and realizing new requirements which further enriches connected solution design to derive better outcomes.

Optimization can happen during every phase viz- monitoring, condition and predictive based maintenance. We called this out as a separate phase as this is an important activity to track on how applying IoT optimizes the current process and the connected products. For instance, using the outcome of predictive maintenance, one can understand failure patterns better and look at corrective ways to schedule services across the globe and order spare parts effectively and in turn optimize the supply chain process.

Going back to the elevator use case, if the elevator is fully occupied and it stops at multiple floors due to passengers wanting to enter, only to find that there is no room to enter. This can annoy passengers who are inside and outside of the elevator. These kinds of pattern (which are not failure conditions) can be detected as part of monitoring phase and therefore it can be optimized by creating a rule to not stop at floors when load is full other than the floors selected by the passengers inside the elevator and notifying passengers waiting for the elevator with the appropriate status. To inspect the user has already taken another elevator, sensors can be applied to track the movement and presence of persons on each floors and share the status at runtime, which is picked up by the incoming elevator and to not stop at the corresponding floor.

Take another example of various 100 storey buildings (in future tall sky scrapers would be quite common), how would a system optimize elevators to ensure maximum passenger satisfaction and least waiting time for passengers taking the elevators, fewer stops per trip and an organized traffic flow to prevent crowding of passengers. These are the cases where optimization and innovation can play an important part and that would mean looking at the elevator IoT solution holistically and not just relying only on data provided by the elevators. It would mean determining connected dots like passenger movements, crowd density at each floors, or even devising smarter algorithms to utilize the data available and suggest optimized steps/routes to the elevator system.

As we move into the future of a connected world, we would see various such use cases which primarily focuses on customer satisfaction and employing new innovations to solve existing problem using the connected information.

Connecting 'connected solutions'
In a connected world, the real innovation would happen on how the data from one connected system would be used by other connected systems and come up with new business models that we haven't thought so far.

For example, let's assume the elevator manufacturing company relies on a third-party vendor for their logistics and shipment of machinery and spare parts. Getting real-time visibility into the moving parts across the globe along with the external factors could help plan the contingency better. For instance, if it takes X amount of additional time to get spare parts from Y location as compared to Z location, but due to real-time weather insight integrated system, reporting extreme weather conditions at Y location for next 3 days, it's better to order spare parts from Z location to reach on time. The distance from Z location can be further optimized based on real-time notifications from traffic systems that can provide an alternate route to the manufacturing plant. Here insights from the logistics aggregation company are offered as the value added services to manufacturing systems.

Take another example of passengers waiting for an elevator, what is the best way to keep the passengers engaged and satisfied and not grumble about the delay. A customer after checking-in to the smart connected hotel and waiting for the elevator for few minutes and later having too many stops to reach at his 90th floor, in one way can be engaged by providing complimentary vouchers for the delay on his Smartphone (through beacons and hotel smart apps on mobile) or through his hotel room card (which is digitized and provide various information) or a call as soon as he reaches his room. In that way, the customer would get the sense of being instantly connected and feel that the hotel acknowledged the delay and cared about it.

Take another example of how data from the connected car solution can be used to derive real values like, traffic management, public safety, fleet management, after sales service and industries like insurance that would tap into the data and devise 'pay per use' model based on actual usage of the car and based on driving/behaviour pattern of the driver. The insurance underwriting process would be changed to take into account these various connected parameters to quote the insurance premium. Insurance companies might also provide various value added services like tying up with service vendors for after sales services or providing just in time insurance for a second person driving the car. Privacy and security can pose a challenge, but they can be effectively handled through service level agreements between car broker/owner and insurance companies.

The current generation does not hesitate to share information on social media. Sometimes sharing information can be tricky but often times you would want to do that to improve your experience with the connected world as every smart business then will be able to provide personalized service based on your personal preference or characteristic. It will bring out positive outcomes and benefit at large and will be appreciated by the same people thereby creating a framework of connected people and business.

In the next section, we will talk about a couple of use cases. We call this as start-up use cases, where start-ups and small organizations are tapping into IoT to create new innovative products from scratch. We would cover two such use cases – connected car and connected home.

Connected Car

Before we deep dive into connected car use case, let's understand a vehicle in the context of IoT. A vehicle can be viewed as a complex system comprising of various subsystems like engines, wheels, doors, brakes, etc. employing many sensors, actuators which are typically controlled by many embedded software devices called an electronic control unit (ECU). Similar to our manufacturing use cases for an elevator, the vehicle subsystems needs to be monitored and serviced through condition and predictive-based maintenance and can employ IoT to derive these insights. As the user is now directly associated to his vehicle, new insights and business models can be derived through the connected vehicle solution. We will discuss more about it in the coming sections.

Let's first start with a formal definition of a connected car. As per Wikipedia – "A connected car is a car that is equipped with Internet access, and usually also with a wireless local area network. This allows the car to share internet access with other devices both inside as well as outside the vehicle."

From a hardware perspective, the car can connect to the internet, through built-in telematics boxes which connect to the internet usually through GSM module (or through Bluetooth or WI-FI tethering via your Smartphone if telematics box supports its) and it's tightly integrated with the car system. The other means of connecting the car is to plug-in a device to the OBD (on board diagnostics) port of the car to extract the vehicle data. The device can have an in-built GSM module or rely on internet connection from the Smartphone through WI-FI, Bluetooth or a USB cable. If you search for the term "OBD" in Amazon you would see tons of manufacturers providing OBD devices which can plug into any car OBD port.

Note - OBD 2 port would be generally available in all modern cars, however you still might have exceptions, so it's better to check your car manual for support (for instance, from 1996, all cars in the US were required to be OBD II equipped, while in India it was mandated from mid of 2013)

IoT Strategy

Let's talk about the connected car use case. With millions of cars without pre-fitted telemetry devices, a hypothetical start-up company thought of exploiting the area of connected car. The same technology from high end cars can be made available at fraction of cost with various value added services. The start-up company decided to target the following use cases:

Hardware Devices

- Providing OBD 2 Port device connector (sourcing OBD II device and adding connectivity options)

Software Services

- Location Tracking

- Real-time performance monitoring of the car
- Condition based maintenance
- Predictive maintenance
- Pre-shipped performance events (change car oil, low tire pressure) + location based services (nearest available service station)
- Creating custom alerts (geo-fencing, high-speed driving, weather data)
- Driver assistance
- Behaviour analysis of the driver
- Recommendation based on driving patterns
- Speak to me (understand your car better)
- Connected solutions - Integration with home automation systems (especially for individual owners), after sales services, remote diagnostics, usage based Insurance, service repair discounts, etc.

The above use cases are applicable to both individuals as well as fleet management companies who could monitor cabs remotely, create alerts for driver speed, analyze driver's behaviour pattern, issue smart invoices based on maps, wait time and actual distance covered.

Hardware Devices

Instead of manufacturing or making devices, the start-up company partners and sources OBD 2 devices directly from manufacturers. Using OBD 2 device, it adds the connectivity code to connect to their cloud IoT platform and transformation code to transform OBD II port data into a customized binary format to minimize the size of data being transferred. The device supports various connectivity options like GSM, 4G LTE modules or relies on internet connection from smart devices through various protocols like Bluetooth, WI-FI or a USB connector. The start-up company decides to build its own customized IoT platform, instead of using services from platform providers. We would talk about one such open source IoT platform stack in next chapter, along with various commercial IoT offerings.

Software Services

The software services listed earlier are developed and deployed as cloud services. Primarily the OBD 2 data and GPS location is made available continuously to the IoT platform in a customized compressed format (think of this a zipped JSON format). Let's inspect some of the information available as part of the OBD port. The values can be retrieved by using the PIDs (Parameter Ids) codes from OBD II port. For instance, to retrieve the vehicle speeds, the standard PID 0D code needs to be used. Some of the information that can be retrieved are:

- Vehicle speed
- Engine RPM
- Diagnostic trouble codes (generic set of codes, but extended by car manufacture's to add their own diagnostic code)
- Coolant temperature
- Air flow rate
- Absolute Throttle Position
- Absolute load value
- Fuel status
- Fuel pressure
- Type pressure
- Battery voltage

The above is only a minimal set of data from the car. Your car is already equipped with hundreds of sensors and with car now being connected; the data generated through the car is being utilized for various other use cases.

Once the OBD and GSP data is available to the IoT core platform, the platform can start consuming it. We would not go in depth about the IoT core platform and more details can be found in the Chapter 1 where we talked about IoT stack. To explain in simple steps, our IoT core platform would read the continuous stream of vehicle data, uncompress the same, persist and analyze the data, execute the required cloud services (condition monitoring, rules, behaviour analysis) and notify the user to his mobile device. A mobile application or web based application is provided to the user to view the data in real-time offered by various services. In Chapter 3, we would talk about how to realize the connected car use case using commercial cloud IoT offerings. Given below are the set of use cases with brief implementation details and how the data can be visualized in a mobile application:

Location Tracking: Provides a map view and location of the car on mobile or web application.

Real-time performance monitoring of the car: Provides real-time graphical and tabular view of the performance data of the car from OBD port

Condition based maintenance: We discussed this earlier with the manufacturing use case. The same approach is applicable for a vehicle, to detect utilization, detect anomaly (faults from normal deviations) and detect if maintenance is required and provide alerts.

Predictive maintenance: We also discussed this earlier with the manufacturing use case. This phase performs predictive maintenance activity of the vehicle using the various approaches discussed earlier as part of the manufacturing process.

Pre-shipped events: Events and rules shipped as part of the initial software and events executed till date and action taken. These are used as part of condition-based maintenance.

Create custom rules and action: Custom rules and event created by the user or the fleet manager (managing the fleet of cars). Rules are basically IF – THEN statements, For instance, if a car is driven by teenager during a specified time interval, the following rule can be created -

IF vehicle speed > 80 km/h and time between 4:00 – 6:00 pm, trigger an SMS.

IF GPS coordinates > geo-fencing coordinates, trigger an SMS.

The second rule is also applicable for fleet managers managing the fleets to track that vehicle don't go beyond a certain boundary or a mapped region due to cross region license restrictions.

Driver assistance: This feature provides various assistance to the driver, like route planning which can minimize fuel consumption or advising the user to not take the regular route due to weather conditions and suggest alternatives.

Driver behaviour analysis: Classifies the driver's ability over a period of time based on the vehicle data (vehicle speed, RPM, throttle position, etc.), idling, accelerometer (tracking rapid lane changes), brake pressure, accelerator pedal position, GPS data (GPS calculated vehicle speed) and driver past history.

The parameters can be fed to a machine learning model which can then classify the driver as – novice, unsafe, neutral, assertive or aggressive.

Tip - Standard OBD II protocol doesn't provide parameters like brake pressure, accelerator pedal position, but it's generally provided by car manufacturers through custom parameter ids. The OBD hardware device should know the parameter ids to extract the relevant value.

Recommendation based on driving patterns: This involves analysis the driver driving patterns over a period of time and providing recommendations on how best to drive the car and utilize the capabilities of the car. For instance, suggesting how to save fuel based on driving patterns (driving at second gear constantly in a geared car), less use of brakes and slowing down the accelerator instead during speed breakers or avoiding sharp turns and yielding at specific locations (tracked via GPS, accelerometer and steering angles).

Speak on: This feature provides value added services where you can speak to a car using natural language and car responds to questions about car features or provide recommendations based on the data gathered from above use cases. Imagine this being a smart SIRI system which is optimized for the connected car and understand the context of the connected car to answer the question effectively.

Connecting connected solutions: Here we will see how data from the connected car can be used by other connected systems. We list some of the use cases below -

- After Sales services – This use case involves how after sales services and maintenance activity would change for providing better service maintenance and monitoring based on actual usage and identify car break down before and suggest corrective action. We went through the set of elevator manufacturing use cases earlier and same is applicable for maintenance activity for a connected car.
- Usage-based insurance – This use case involves how Insurance companies can utilize the data from a connected car like actual utilization and driver behaviour analysis for creating personalized car insurance quotes.
- Integration with connected systems – This use cases provides rules and connectivity via exposed APIs in a secure way to connect with other connected systems – like home automation. For instance, starting your coffee machine as soon as your car reaches x distance from your home or reserving a parking lot before your car reaches the shopping mall. The other use cases are using the connected car data for autonomous driving, smarter cities (traffic management) etc.

Connected Home

Connected home is about an idea of creating a home where virtually everything is connected to the internet, from doors to lighting system, appliances (television, refrigerator, washing machine etc.) and everything you can imagine of is connected and controlled remotely.

Before we delve into the use case, let's understand the current landscape of a connected home and challenges that needs to be addressed .The real challenge in a connected home is using a standardized protocol for communication. Current vendors are taking a step in this direction, for instance providing a hub (think this as a device gateway) and a set of compatible devices which can communicate to the central hub. The devices include sensors to detect movements (when people arrive and leave home), vibrations, temperature, switches (to control small appliances like a thermostat) and lighting systems (like bulbs, led, etc.). The protocol used for communication is usually non-standardized, proprietary and low-frequency radio protocol like ZigBee or Z-wave which is typically used by lighting system (bulbs, led etc.)

When we mean non-standardized, we mean that it is not possible to bring a connected TV from a different manufacturer, or a connected washing machine from a different vendor and make it talk to your connected home (or hub we talked about). You don't want to have multiple hubs and manage each one of them independently and some devices might not need a hub and can talk to the cloud platform directly via WI-FI. Everyone is providing a hub model and set of APIs (open source, proprietary) and prompting device manufacturers to build around the APIs for connectivity.

The real use cases are not about providing seamless connectivity, but once connected, what value you want to derive from a connected home. It's not only about home automation, but how would you use the vast amount of data generated to come up with new business models and innovative solutions.

Let's talk about one such case, where you would like to optimize the electricity usage across your home, predict electricity usage for the current month based on actual usage and optimize it for the remaining days in a month and identify patterns and recommendations from the system. Unless you gather data across these connected devices to understand the usage and electric consumption from the devices, it would be difficult to come up with services such as

- Home Electricity Utilization
- Home Electricity Monthly Prediction
- Home Electricity Optimization
- Home Electricity Usage Patterns
- Home Electricity Recommendation Savings
- Self-Optimization – Apply Recommendation

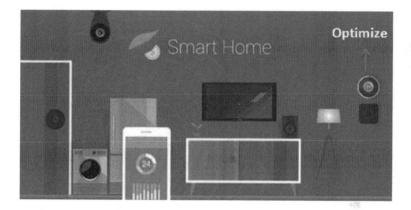

Energy is a valuable resource and even a 10% reduction and savings would mean a lot to consumers as well as to the environment. We still see energy and load shedding happening in places and technology innovations like this could help resolve such problems in near future.

Let's talk about options for seamless integration. One way is making all the devices talk to a common cloud platform and analyze the data, but it has its own challenges. The protocols and data formats would be different for different devices; the devices should be modified to add connectivity code to talk to the common platform and security needs to be looked at holistically. A common device gateways can be used which does this conversion, filters out the data and talks to cloud platform, but it would mean the rest of the devices connects to that common device gateway in a standardized way using a standardized protocol, else the device code needs to be changed to talk to the device gateway. The set of integration challenges would remain, but in future we could see some convergence on a standardized protocol like AllJoyn, or using Google operation system (Brillo) as most smart systems now ships with some android capability (like Smart TV, refrigerators etc.).

IoT is a big ecosystem, and it would not be about one particular IoT platform or using one IoT protocol, but how large volume and variety of data can be consumed, correlated from multiple sources and analyzed to offer better outcomes – like optimization of electricity usage, predictive maintenance for connected components and better after-sales services of connected product to name a few. From an implementation perspective, we are looking at continuous machine learning models which learn from the data and provide optimization. The model updates can happen in near real-time in future, where feedbacks are continuously observed for better optimization.

Partnership would be equally important where a connected TV already have pre-shipped device connectivity to support a particular cloud platform (say Microsoft Azure, IBM Bluemix or Amazon AWS), but you could have one device supporting Azure, other IBM and problem still needs to be resolved, as a System Integrator don't want to add device connectivity code for each device and manage it.

We believe the connected home has a great future and would be part of consumer digital extension, but still it has a long way to go and reap its benefits. Current products do provide connectivity to basic home appliances, tracking movements and behaviour. Home automation is just a start, but real benefits can be seen only when there is seamless connectivity across all the connected products in a home, from doors to lighting systems, to any appliances (television, refrigerator, washing machine). This should be independent of any vendor or supported protocol. More importantly through data analytics, one should be able to derive observations and optimization that can benefit the end consumer. Imagine an effective energy optimization plan derived based on actual usage from a home (keeping security aspects in mind) being shared by other home systems to provide suggestions and patterns on how other home users can optimize their home energy consumption.

Summary

In this chapter, we looked at the application of IoT taking the examples of different industry domains. We went through two set of use cases – one where automation and some instrumentation already exist as in manufacturing domain and other where a connected solution is developed from scratch. We went through various phases in the manufacturing use case and how IoT was incrementally applied to derive the business outcome. At the end, we discussed the connected car and home automation use cases. In the next chapter, we will look at how to realize industry use cases using commercial IoT offerings and open source technologies.

Chapter 3. IoT Implementations

In this chapter, we will look at how to build IoT applications using commercial IoT offerings provided by Microsoft, IBM, and Amazon and even build the strategy for an open source IoT stack.

Let's first understand the various players in building an enterprise IoT application.

Manufacturer

These are manufacturers or maker of connected products. While building a connected product, the main challenge is the design of the connected product and what actionable insights need to be derived from the connected product for delivering the business outcome. The other major challenges include –

- How will the connected product interact with the provided network and platform (cloud) providers?
- What communication protocol needs to be supported?
- Lifecycle and management of the connected product.
- Security considerations of the overall connected solution

Network providers

They provide the backbone infrastructure and networking components for connectivity like IP switches, WLAN, intelligent gateways and scalable topologies for large scale deployments. Imagine a network provider providing the networking infrastructure for smart cities or a secure connectivity across manufacturing plants.

Note – The setting up of intelligent gateways would be a key topology requirement in future. The intelligent gateway should provide local filtering of data and analytics so that only the required information is sent to the next layer. The next layer could be another intelligent gateway or the platform (cloud) provider.

Platform providers

The platform providers provide the software backbone. They provide a scalable messaging infrastructure which devices can connect to using supported protocols and an analytics platform for analyzing large volumes of data to discover insights and predict outcomes. All the IoT software capabilities are usually offered as services over the cloud which can be composed to form an IoT solution.

For instance, a platform provider may provide the following catalog of IoT services:

- Connectivity services to allow millions of devices to be connected in a secured way.
- Data filtering services to filter volumes of data based on business rules.
- Support for various storage types like time series and NoSQL database to store the continuous data.
- Real-time streaming service to stream data from connected devices.
- Tools to build and deploy machine learning models from the data to predict outcomes, detect anomaly etc.
- Integration services to integrate with other backend systems (for example, triggering a workflow order request for spare parts in SAP system based on the outcome of the machine learning model or executing a business process flow).
- Dashboard services for viewing analyzed data and event services to trigger events, alerts like push events to mobiles or SMS to service technicians to fix the problem.

The catalog of IoT services provided by the platform providers will continue to grow in future along with various values added services which would make it easier to build IoT applications.

System Integrator

A System Integrator (SI) would play a key role in building the IoT solution by providing end-to-end integration, standards interoperability, simulation and testing, network operability and identifying bottlenecks, scalability and performance requirements. For instance, in case of manufacturing use cases, the SI could be involved in mapping existing devices, systems including sensors and proprietary protocols with a standardized protocol. SI could also decide how many new devices need to be instrumented.

Apart from solving the integration issues, we feel the real challenge would involve simulation of end to end use case and coping up with innovative solutions. For instance, how to test the design, validate and simulate a smart city model from an end to end perspective right from devices working together and reporting the right data, network traffic simulation to avoid bottlenecks, application and platform scalability, security testing and expected data flow across the system to name a few.

With the context set, the rest of the chapter would focus on specific platform providers .The strategy adopted by platform providers is pretty much the same i.e. providing a cloud platform and set of services for building IoT applications. These categories of cloud computing services are referred to as Platform as a Service (PaaS) which provides a platform to build applications from set of services, test and run applications without worrying about the complexity of maintaining the infrastructure. For instance, the platform provider could provide a pre-configured clustered Node.js service, and the job would be to deploy the node application without worrying about the installation, upgrades, security, scalability and most importantly maintaining the physical servers.

Building application with Microsoft IoT platform

Microsoft provides a cloud computing platform called Azure, which is a growing collection of integrated services like analytics, database, mobile, networking, storage and web - for moving faster, achieving more and saving money.

Microsoft provides a set of IoT services (referred to as Microsoft Azure IoT services) over its Azure platform to help build IoT applications rapidly. Microsoft recently launched the Azure IoT suite (on Sept 29th 2015) which offers pre-configured IoT solutions built on Microsoft's cloud platform and makes it easy to connect devices securely and supports broad set of protocols. We will discuss the Azure IoT suite and its capabilities in detail during the course of the chapter

In the first chapter, we had discussed about a generic Enterprise IoT stack. Following diagram shows how the how components in the Enterprise IoT stack is mapped with Microsoft Azure IoT services.

IoT Stack Mapping for Microsoft IoT

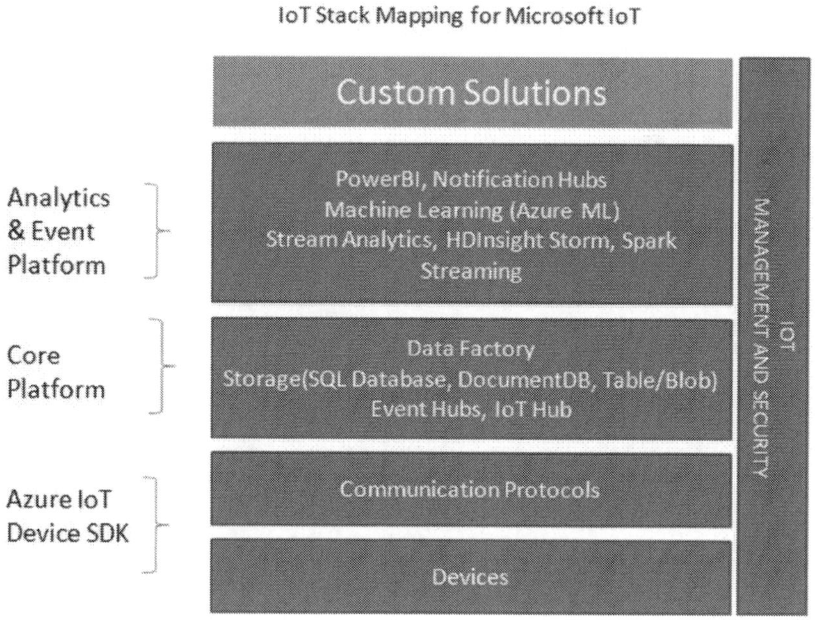

Azure IoT Device SDK

These are device SDK for different platforms like Linux, Android, iOS Windows etc., which makes it easier to get started on any device and connect to Azure IoT platform. These are optional, a device manufacturer can use the APIs to get started quickly or add its own device connectivity code for connecting to Azure platform e.g. using a JavaScript device API for Intel Edison device or an optimized C SDK for a Linux device. The Azure IoT device SDKs is available in GitHub at https://github.com/Azure/azure-iot-sdks. The Azure IoT SDK connects devices to IoT Hub. We will discuss IoT Hub in detail in the following section.

The following shows a C code snippet which uses the C device SDKS to connect to Azure IoT Hub. The template code can also be generated from the following page: https://azure.microsoft.com/en-us/develop/iot/get-started/

```c
staticconstchar* connectionString ="[device connection
string]";
staticchar msgText[1024];
void main(void){
  IoTHUB_CLIENT_HANDLE iotHubClientHandle;
  IoTHUB_MESSAGE_HANDLE message;

/* Create IoT Hub Client instance */
  iotHubClientHandle =
IoTHubClient_CreateFromConnectionString(connectionStrin
g, AMQP_Protocol);

/* Setting Message call back, so we can receive
Commands. */
  IoTHubClient_SetMessageCallback(iotHubClientHandle,
ReceiveMessageCallback,&receiveContext);

/* Now that we are ready to receive commands, let's
send a message */

sprintf_s(msgText,sizeof(msgText),"{\"deviceId\":\"myFi
rstDevice\",\"data\":%.2f}", rand()%4+2);
  message.messageHandle =
IoTHubMessage_CreateFromByteArray((constunsignedchar*)m
sgText, strlen(msgText));
```

```
   IoTHubClient_SendEventAsync(iotHubClientHandle,
message, SendConfirmationCallback,&message);

/* Add your code here ... */

/* When everything is done and the app is closing,
clean up resources */
   IoTHubClient_Destroy(iotHubClientHandle);
}
static IoTHUBMESSAGE_DISPOSITION_RESULT
ReceiveMessageCallback(IoTHUB_MESSAGE_HANDLE
message,void* userContextCallback)
{
constchar* buffer;
   size_t size;

IoTHubMessage_GetByteArray(message,(constunsignedchar**
)&buffer,&size);
(void)printf("Received Message with Data: <<<%.*s>>>&
Size=%d\r\n",(int)size, buffer,(int)size);
/* Some device specific action code goes here... */
return IoTHUBMESSAGE_ACCEPTED;
}
staticvoid
SendConfirmationCallback(IoTHUB_CLIENT_CONFIRMATION_RES
ULT result,void* userContextCallback)
{
   IoTHUB_MESSAGE_HANDLE* message
=(IoTHUB_MESSAGE_HANDLE*)userContextCallback;
(void)printf("Confirmation received for message
tracking id = %d with result = %s\r\n", eventInstance-
>messageTrackingId,
ENUM_TO_STRING(IoTHUB_CLIENT_CONFIRMATION_RESULT,
result));
/* Some device specific action code goes here... */
   IoTHubMessage_Destroy(*message);
}
```

Tip - ConnectTheDots.io is another open source project created by Microsoft which allows devices to connect to Azure platform. It was developed prior to Azure device SDKs and does not use the SDK. Currently it provides connectivity to Event Hubs only, which we would discuss it later.

Azure IoT Hub

Azure IoT Hub, a part of the recently released Azure IoT suite, is a fully managed bidirectional device to cloud connectivity bus, providing device management, device security and identity and MQTT protocol support apart from HTTP/AMQP.

Note - The MQTT protocol support is handled through the protocol gateway pattern that we had discussed as part of Enterprise IoT stack - core platform layer section in Chapter 1.

Azure IoT Hub provides complete device access through the use of its device identity registry. It provides per device authentication and secure bi-direction connectivity between devices and IoT Hub. The IoT Hub can also integrate with your custom device registry through the use of a token service to create a device-scoped token for secure communication with IoT Hub.

Each Azure IoT Hub allows certain number of devices which can be simultaneously connected along with frequency of message that can be transmitted per day by the devices. Scaling Azure IoT Hub is a matter of adding additional IoT Hub units. Azure IoT Hub is capable of handling millions of simultaneously connected devices and millions of events per seconds. For details on IoT Hub units and pricing, kindly refer to this link - https://azure.microsoft.com/en-us/pricing/details/iot-hub/.

Azure IoT Hub classifies the bi-direction messaging capability as device-to-cloud and cloud-to-device messaging. The IoT Hub implements 'at least once' delivery guarantees for both device-to-cloud and cloud-to-device messaging. It provides local storage of messages of up to 7 days for device-to-cloud messages and a dedicated device queue for each connected devices for storing cloud-to-device messages that are consumed by the devices securely. This eliminates the overhead of creating separate queues for sending messages back to devices.

Azure IoT Hub and rest of the Azure services parameters can be configured through the Azure Portal. Following shows a snapshot of a single Azure IoT Hub unit. We will discuss the configuration in detail in the implementation section.

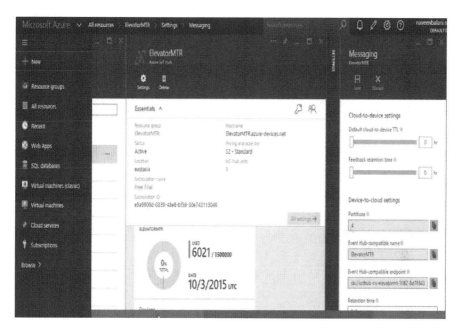

Event Hubs

Event Hubs is a highly scalable publish-subscribe event processing service. Event Hubs is a part of Azure Service Bus platform which is capable of collecting millions of messages per second with low latency and high reliability, which can be stored for further analysis (historical analysis by machine learning models, auditing, batch processing etc.) or acted upon directly by stream analytics services. Event Hubs support HTTP and AMQP protocol. Prior to the release of IoT Hub, Event Hubs was used primarily to support IoT applications. However, Event Hubs only support connecting devices to cloud and does not support per device secure identity out of the box, like the IoT Hub. The Azure device SDKs that we talked about earlier which makes it easier to connect variety of device platforms, supports connectivity to IoT Hub only, while device connecting to Event Hubs needs to rely on AMQP and HTTP interfaces or use the open source project ConnectTheDots.io. IoT Hub is specifically designed to handle IoT use cases, taking into account device connectivity, identity and secure bi-direction communication between devices and IoT Hub. It is therefore recommended to use IoT Hub for IoT applications. In a typical enterprise IoT application you would use IoT Hub and Event Hubs in conjunction, where IoT Hub would handle secure device connectivity and hand off messages to Event Hubs for real-time processing.

Storage

The storage comprises of using various options for storing the continuous streams of data. The storage options includes SQL Database, DocumentDB (NoSQL) or highly scalable, high performance Blobs, Tables and Queues. You also have a choice of using HBase on HDInsight. HDInsight is an Apache Hadoop based services on Azure cloud. As mentioned earlier, IoT Hub provides the retention of messages for guaranteed delivery, but you would typically use a dedicated storage option to store the messages for further analysis and historical computations. Typically you would use DocumentDB, high performance Blob or HBase based on volume of data that needs to be stored and analyzed

Azure Data Factory

Azure Data Factory service lets you ingest data from diverse sources (cloud as well as on-premise sources), transform the data and make it consumable for your application. Not all applications may require the use of Data Factory, but we would like to mention this specifically, as your application might need to be integrated with diverse set of data sources (and even on-premise databases) to correlate or to augment information provided by device data.

Azure Stream Analytics

The Azure Stream Analytics provides real-time stream processing of millions of events per second, enabling you to compare and correlate multiple real-time streams, query data using familiar SQL language and create real-time dashboard and alerts.

Note - The data from Event Hubs can be directly consumed and analysed by Azure Stream Analytics, without actually storing the data using the storage options.

Microsoft Azure also supports open source streaming solutions like Apache Storm and Apace Spark Streaming as part of the HDInsight services. PaaS vendors should provide support for open source streaming platform solutions and make it easier to implement custom streaming applications without the user worrying about its configuration, scalability or security. One can also look at Azure Data Lake storage service that stores data of any size and allows performing all types of processing and analytics. More details about Azure Data Lake can be found at https://azure.microsoft.com/en-us/solutions/data-lake/.

Machine Learning

Azure Machine Learning provides a visual way to build machine learning model that supports R and Python custom packages, pre-built algorithms and enables us to build custom model by adding custom code based on the requirements. In future, we envision support for more machine language libraries and expect this to be a market place for machine learning models. These learning models will be specifically targeted towards IoT use cases like predictive maintenance for vehicle, refrigerators etc. and you might have various such variants and pricing based on the optimization and accuracy levels of the machine learning models.

Events and Reporting

These services include sending notifications, like an alert to mobile phones using push notification via the Notification Hubs service or invoking an action using Azure APIs, for instance calling the on-premise application (like a custom workflow exposed as web services) through Logic Apps. Logic Apps lets you automate processes using visual tools and provide connectors for easily integrating disparate data sources from cloud to on-premises. You could also use PowerBI cloud service which allows visualizing and analyzing the data using powerful and flexible dashboards. The Azure Stream Analytics can feed real-time data events into PowerBI and you can design dashboards which use the data and can be updated at runtime.

For the PowerBI and Azure Stream Analytics integration, while creating the Azure stream job instance you need to select PowerBI as the output of the streaming job and provide the required settings. We would go over the details in the implementation section. For the data to be made available to PowerBI instance you need to create a query in the Query Tab of the stream job instance and output of the query would be made available in PowerBI. You can then use the data to build dashboards.

Note - You need to have a Microsoft Power BI account subscription to use it with Azure Stream Analytics.

Custom Solutions

These are an end to end IoT solutions developed using Azure services. Azure also provides bunch of other services that can be used for building

IoT solutions apart from Azure IoT services like – the mobile push service to send an alert based on the analysis, the Redis Cache for high throughput and low latency data access or using the Azure APIs for building custom applications to consume the information from Azure Portal. You can find all these services in the product menu option of Azure website at https://azure.microsoft.com/en-us/.

Note- Most of the cloud services mentioned were not specifically designed for handling IoT requirements, like Event Hubs and Azure Stream Analytics which can be used for other requirements as well like real-time fraud detection, while products like IoT Hub are specially designed to address IoT requirements. We expect more such offerings in future tailored towards realizing IoT use cases.

Implementation Overview

Let's understand how to use these services, by taking the example of the connected car use case we discussed earlier. The connected car device manufacturer ties it up with Microsoft Azure platform for using its cloud services to realize the various use cases we discussed in connected car section using the Azure platform.

Hardware and Connecivity

The connected car device manufacturer takes care of hardware devices and network provisioning (using GSM module or using internet connectivity via Bluetooth or WI-FI from Smartphones). The device manufacturer provides reliable connectivity and optimum network utilization (2G/3G/4G LTE). To communicate with the Azure platform, the device comes pre-installed with the connectivity code to the Azure platform using the Azure Device SDKs.

The pre-shipped device comes up with highest level of security, both on the hardware and software side and set of unique codes (device ids) with ensures only authorized devices can talk to Azure platform. The device manufacturer has provisioned all the devices (as part of its device design and provision step) using Azure Device Management APIs which are exposed as HTTP REST endpoints. The device manufacturer also implements commands like pause, start, stop, diagnose device which can be controlled through the IoT Hub. The device software uses the Azure Device SDK to transmit the data from the connected car securely to the Azure IoT platform using JSON format over AMQP protocol. The device also provides a display unit which is used to display usage information and communication from Azure IoT platform.

IoT Solution Strategy

The solution strategy comprises of using the Azure IoT services we described earlier to build the connected car IoT application.

In order to receive messages on Azure platform and eventually start processing the same, there are a bunch of activities that needs to be done. Our solution uses two approaches to process the incoming data – real-time and batch analysis. The real-time approach processes the continuous stream of data arriving at IoT Hub from devices that includes taking the required action at runtime (like raising an alert, sending data back to devices or invoking a third party service for maintenance order), while batch analysis includes storing the data for further analysis and running complex analytics jobs or using existing Hadoop jobs for data analysis. The batch analysis would also be used for developing and training the machine learning models iteratively and then using these deployed models at runtime for real-time actions.

The following image shows the Azure Management portal where a set of task needs to be executed.

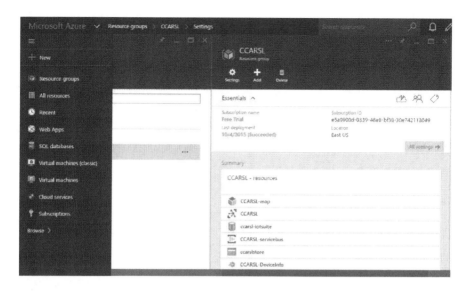

Following are the high level steps that needs to be performed in Azure
Management Portal

1. Create Resource Group
2. Create an IoT Hub
3. Create Device Identity
4. Provision Hardware devices
5. Create Storage Service
6. Create Azure Stream Analytics Jobs
7. Create Event Hubs
8. Create PowerBI dashboards
9. Create Notification Hubs
10. Create Machine Learning (ML) model

We had discussed all of the above capabilities earlier except the Resource
Group. A Resource Group basically is a container for all resources related
to a specific application which uses the same subscription information and
is hosted in the same location. We create one resource group for
connected car and all the resources would use this resource group.

We would not go over the configuration steps in detail, but summarize one execution flow for the connected car use case which uses the above resources.

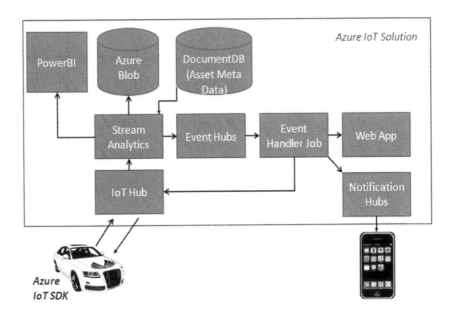

Real-time Flow

The IoT Hub receives the data from the connected car device over AMQP protocol. Once the data is received, the stream of data is consumed by Azure Stream Analytic jobs. As part of configuring the Azure Stream Analytics job, you specify the input source as IoT Hub and specify the input format (JSON) and encoding (UTF-8). This would stream all data from IoT Hub to this Azure Stream Analytics job. As part of output configuration you specify where you want to store the output of the job, for instance Blob Storage, Event Hubs, PowerBI etc. Following image shows the list of output options:

Add an output to your job

- SQL Database
- Blob storage
- Event Hub
- Power BI   PREVIEW
- Table storage
- Service Bus Queue
- Service Bus Topic
- DocumentDB

Missing an output sink? Let us know! (Powered by UserVoice - Privacy Policy)

In the Query Tab on the Azure Stream Analytics job, you specify the query (SQL like queries) which works on the input data and produces the output. The output (in JSON format) is delivered to the output channel.

For our connected car scenario, we create two Azure Stream Analytics jobs. For the first job, we specify the input as IoT Hub. The query is to select all the incoming data. There are two output configuration specified, one output dumps the data into Azure Blob for further analysis and other dumps the data into PowerBI for creating dashboard. Following image shows the snippet of Query view:

ccarsoln-telemetry

Need help with your query? Check out some of the most common Stream Analytics query patterns here.

query

```
1  WITH
2      [StreamData] AS (
3      SELECT
4          *
5      FROM
6          [IoTHubStream]
7      WHERE
8          [ObjectType] IS NULL |)
9  SELECT
10     *
11 INTO
12     [Telemetry]
13 FROM
14     [StreamData]
15
```

For the second Azure Stream Analytics Job, we create two inputs, the first input is IoT Hub and other is the Asset DB which contains the asset metadata. For the query, we create condition based rules which trigger if conditions are not met (like speed >100 km/hour, low engine oil, low tire pressure). The Azure Stream Analytics rules correlates asset metadata and runtime data of the connected car to trigger conditions based on asset specifications. The asset specification contains the asset details and ideal permissible limit of the asset – be it car engine, tyre pressure, engine oil etc. This is simple condition based maintenance. The result from the rules is stored in output storage. The output is stored in an Event Hubs for further processing by various applications.

Note – We had talk about asset management phase while discussing the IoT use cases in Chapter 2. The same requirements apply for connected car also.

A custom Event Handler is created which acts as a consumer and picks up the data from Event Hubs and uses the Notification Hubs APIs to push high priority events to mobiles. The handler also sends updates to web dashboards and sends the message back to the IoT Hub device queue for that device using the device id. The connected car device receives the notification on the device dashboard.

Offline Process

Now, let's discuss the offline process. The offline process is mainly used for batch processing, analyzing volumes of data, correlating data from multiple sources and complex data flows. The other scenario is developing machine learning models from these various data sets, training and testing iteratively to build models which can predict or classify with reasonable accuracy.

Building Machine Learning Models

Building machine learning models is an iterative process and it involves a bunch of tasks as depicted in the diagram below.

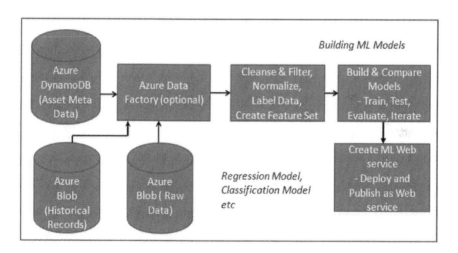

For the connected car solution, we would build two machine learning models – one for predictive maintenance and other for driver behaviour analysis.

Following list shows high level steps to build machine learning model using Azure ML. The steps listed below are generic and applicable for building any machine learning model.

- Select the data sources that you would need for building the model. In the connected car scenario, our data sources are Azure Blob (raw vehicle data), Azure Dynamo DB (Asset Meta Data) and a second Azure Blob which contains historical records for vehicle maintenance and driver classification. In absence of the historical records, it is still possible to build predictive models with unsupervised learning techniques and later correlating the outputs manually and deriving insights. The entire process tends to be very complex. Most of the tools doesn't support this methodology and expect you to provide labelled data (input and output). In future, data generated from the connected product would be one key valuable asset and you would see various data providers providing such historical records (like trends) for analysis.
- The Azure Data Factory is an optional data service added to the design to transfer and analyze the raw data and create data process pipelines to make the data consumable. The Data Factory in particular is useful if you need to integrate with multiple systems and perform data processing to arrive at the desired output.
- The third step is about preparing the data to be used by the model. This involves cleaning and filtering the data, normalizing the data, creating labelled inputs for classification and most importantly creating relevant feature sets based on the use case requirements. Selecting a feature set and building the model is a complex exercise and requires thorough understanding and expertise on machine learning and it's outside the scope of this book. Preparation of data is the most crucial and time consuming step in building the model. As part of this step you would also create train and test set. You would train the model using the train set and test your model iteratively using the test set. Azure ML provides visual composition tools to enable prepare the data. Azure ML is available over the web and you can execute the entire end-to-end process without installing any additional software.

- Once the data is prepared, you start building the model using Azure ML by selecting the type of model (regression, classification etc.) and algorithms associated with it and use the data from the previous step. For instance, for regression model, you could use neural network regression, decision forest algorithms etc. You can evaluate all the models to understand which one performs better for your data set. As mentioned this is an iterative step. For the connected car solution, we will perform predictive maintenance using regression algorithms and for behaviour analysis we use multi-class classification. The regression model output would be a confidence score that indicates whether maintenance is required for the equipment or not. For behaviour analysis, the model could be classified as aggressive, neutral etc.
- Next step is publishing the machine learning model as the web service, so it can be consumed by the application though an API call.

As mentioned earlier, the real challenge is building the machine learning model and training the model to predict a reasonable outcome. This requires a significant effort and training to get a reasonable prediction over a period of time. Azure Stream Analytics lets you combine data from multiple streams, so you could combine real-time and historical data and arrive at an outcome. For instance, you can also combine streams to detect anomaly in real-time through machine learning models.

Currently there are no pre-built machine learning models available for industries and hence an offline process is required to build the model iteratively. In future, we envision machine learning models would be available as services for each industry like predictive maintenance for vehicles or specific machinery types. All then you have to do is provide the data to the machine learning models for prediction. We had discussed this concept in the earlier chapter where we had talked about Solution Template in Chapter 1.

Integrating Machine Learning Models with Real-time Flow

Once our machine learning model is ready, as the last step we integrate the machine learning model with the runtime flow as shown below.

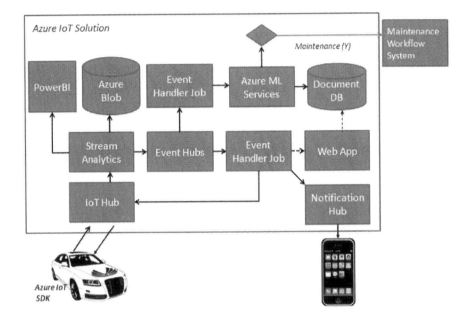

We added one more event handler to the existing flow, which calls our predictive model Azure ML service through the API. Based on the response, if maintenance is required the event handler invokes an external request to maintenance workflow system to initiate a work order for repair. The integration of driver behaviour analysis is pretty much the same and in this case the output goes to mobile and web instead of a maintenance request.

Microsoft Azure IoT Suite

Azure IoT suite which was released recently (29th September 2015), is a cloud-based offering with pre-configured solutions that address common Internet of Things scenarios, so you can capture and analyze untapped data to transform your business.

Azure IoT Suite is a set of IoT services that we discussed earlier in this course of chapter, along with pre-configured solutions, like remote monitoring and predictive maintenance, which makes it easier to get started on your IoT projects. We had discussed these use cases in detail in earlier chapter. The following shows a snapshot of Azure IoT suite pre-configured solution.

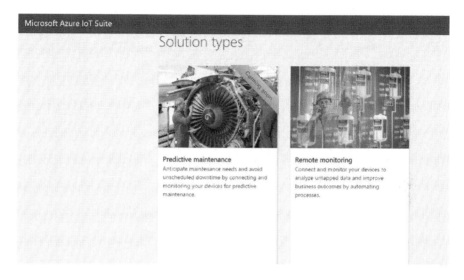

The following image show what Azure services are included as part of the remote monitoring solution. As you see the solution comprised of Azure IoT Hub, Azure Stream Analytics, Azure DocumentDB etc. and host of other services that we described in this chapter.

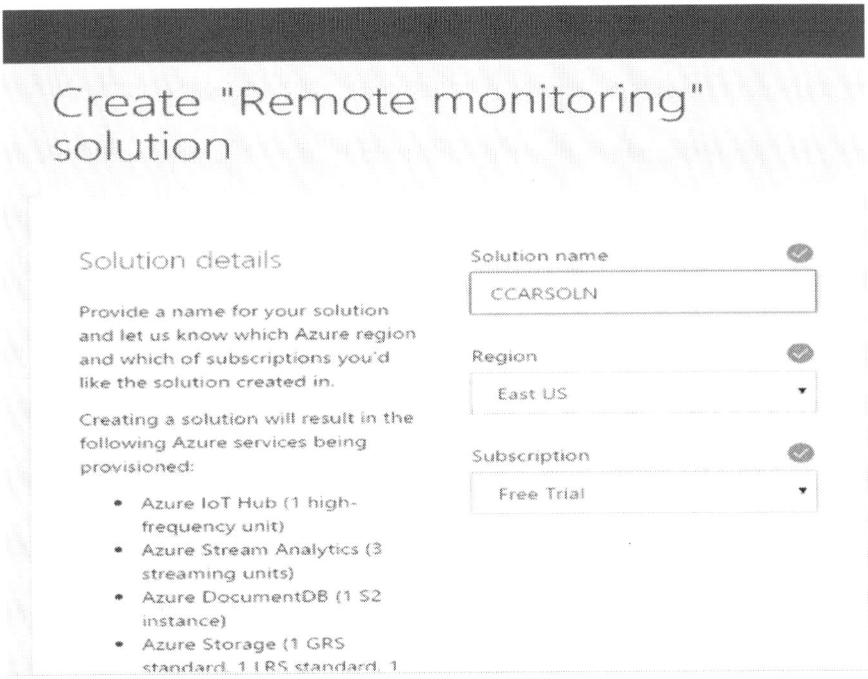

Create "Remote monitoring" solution

Solution details

Provide a name for your solution and let us know which Azure region and which of subscriptions you'd like the solution created in.

Creating a solution will result in the following Azure services being provisioned:

- Azure IoT Hub (1 high-frequency unit)
- Azure Stream Analytics (3 streaming units)
- Azure DocumentDB (1 S2 instance)
- Azure Storage (1 GRS standard, 1 LRS standard, 1

Solution name

CCARSOLN

Region

East US

Subscription

Free Trial

The following figure shows the remote monitoring solution in action, which provides a map view of where the devices are located, alarm history details which lists down alerts, rules and actions executed so far and a graph view which plots the humidity and temperature recordings for the selected device.

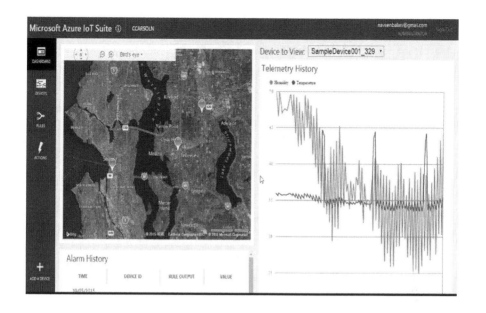

The concept of pre-configured solutions somewhat maps to the solution template component that we had discussed in the solutions section as part of our IoT stack. The solutions here are provided as part of Microsoft Azure IoT Suite. To build IoT applications for a specific industry, instead of starting from scratch, the pre-configured solutions could provide a quick start, which then later can be customized to suit the requirements.

Tip – For details on Azure IoT predictive maintenance preconfigured solution and its architecture, kindly visit this link - https://azure.microsoft.com/en-in/documentation/articles/iot-suite-predictive-walkthrough/ . The predictive maintenance solution also includes an end to end integration with Azure Machine Learning service.

Building application with IBM IoT Platform

In this section, we would look at how to realize the IoT use case using IBM IoT platform. IBM provides the Internet of Things Foundation (IoTF) offering which is a fully managed, cloud-hosted service that makes it simple to derive value from Internet of Things (IoT) devices. Together with IBM PaaS platform (Bluemix), you can rapidly build IoT applications from the catalog of services available in Bluemix. The catalog of services for an IoT application typically includes – storage services, rules, analytics services, stream analytics and machine learning. We went through this earlier when we talked about Microsoft IoT stack in detail. The strategy adopted by Microsoft and IBM is pretty much the same.

Note – IBM Bluemix is an implementation of IBM's Open Cloud Architecture based on Cloud Foundry. Cloud Foundry is an open source industry standard platform for building cloud applications in a vendor neutral way.

In the first chapter, we had discussed about a generic Enterprise IoT stack. The following shows our representation on how the IBM IoT services can be mapped to our generic Enterprise IoT stack.

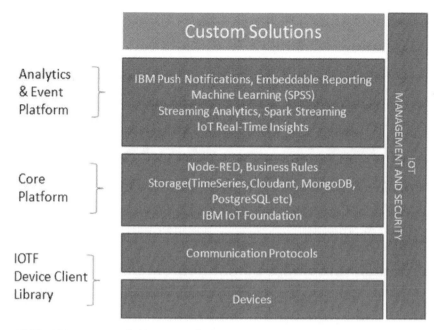

IOTF - IBM Internet of Things Foundation

Let's go through the components in details

IoTF Device Client Library

These are client libraries which makes it easier to connect devices to the IoTF Platform. The IoTF provides client library in Python, Java, Embedded C, Node.js and C#. For details on the client library API, please look at https://docs.internetofthings.ibmcloud.com/libraries/programmingguides.html

IBM IoTF also offers device recipes which provide code and detail steps to connect various devices to IBM IoTF using MQTT protocol. (IBM IoTF currently provides support for only MQTT protocol.). The device recipe is contributed by IBM, third party vendors and the community. Following shows a snapshot of recipes being currently offered by IBM and its IoT ecosystem.

81 recipes in total

Connect a Raspberry Pi to
Internet of Things Foundation

By Vikki Paterson
February 25, 2015

CC2650 SimpleLink™
Bluetooth® Smart BLE
SensorTag

By rdmonk

National Instruments LabVIEW
for the IoT Foundation

By Steve Haskey
March 24, 2015

You can also build your own device recipe using the open source Eclipse
based Paho library (http://www.eclipse.org/paho/) which provides client
implementations of MQTT and MQTT-SN protocol for requires devices.
You need to pick up a supported Paho library, like a .Net for Windows 10
devices or C client for devices supporting C programming language.

Following is the code snippet that can be used by devices to connect to
IBM IoTF using IoTF Node.js library:

```
var Client = require("ibmIoTF").IoTFDevice;
var config ={
"org":"organization",
"id":"deviceId",
"type":"deviceType",
"auth-method":"token",
"auth-token":"authToken"
};

var deviceClient =new Client(config);
deviceClient.connect();

deviceClient.on("connect",function(){

var myQosLevel=2// QOS, message is delivered exactly
once
client.publish("status","json",'{"d" : { "cpu" : 60,
"mem" : 50 }}', myQosLevel);
```

```
});
```

Internet of Things Foundation (IoTF)

IBM Internet of Things Foundation (IoTF) lets you connect a wide variety of devices securely and collect and manage data in time series. IoTF follows the pub-sub model, where you create topics for communication between publishers (like devices) and subscribers. IoTF also addresses security by providing secure channel for devices to connect to IoTF using MQTT over TLS. It provides device management infrastructure like web dashboards for managing and monitoring the data usage, providing set of APIs for registering the devices, getting list of connected devices, events generated by devices and device diagnostic logs. The APIs can be accessed at: https://docs.internetofthings.ibmcloud.com/swagger/v0002.html (this is version 2 of the API at the time of writing this book).

To get started with IoTF, you select the Internet of Things service in Bluemix and create an instance. This will assign an organization unit and ID, which is a unique ID provided by the IoTF System. Organizations acts like a domain where data is only accessible from devices and applications in that domain. Once devices are registered, devices and API keys are bound to that organization. When an application connects to the IoTF service using an API key, it registers with the organization that "owns" the API key. Using this combination it makes it impossible for other devices and applications which are not part of the same organization to communicate with each other. IoTF also provides storage of device data based on terms specified (in months). The following image shows a snapshot of IoTF, depicting one registered device.

Once you register the device, you get an authorization code which is used for connecting the device to the IoTF. As part of device registration process, you can also store the device metadata like serial number, firmware or custom attributes in JSON, which can be used further for device management activities.

IoTF allows for firmware updates, reboot and factory reset commands which need to be supported and executed by the device. Think of this as set of device commands which a device agents runs on the device when it receives the command input from IoTF dashboard. You specify the command actions through the Action tab in the dashboard or through the device command APIs. The APIs supported by IoTF and sample message formats are listed at the URL - https://IoTF.readthedocs.org/en/latest/api/device_management.html.

The IBM Internet of Things Foundation platform is powered by IBM's core products and services which includes MessageSight (rapid bi-directional messaging), Informix TimeSeries (time series database), Data Power Gateway (secure gateway and integration), Cloudant (NoSQL for storing device metadata), WebSphere Application server Liberty Core (runtime for IoTF dashboard/webapps) and a host of other open source projects.

Tip - To try a one minute quick demo to see MQTT accelerometer events from your phone to IoTF foundation, visit https://console.ng.Bluemix.net/solutions/iot (look for play now button in 'Try it out now with our cool sample app' section.)

Storage

IoTF platform by default provides data storage capability and time series view of the data from devices. But it's better to use a separate storage for storing, accessing and analyzing volumes of historical data which can be used by services and applications that needs to consume or augment the data with other data sources. For choice of storage, Bluemix offers a variety of scalable database storage options like MongoDB, PostgreSQL, Cloudant NoSQL, IBM DB2, ObjectStorage and Informix Time Series data. The choice of using a specific database depends on the use case requirements, volume of data that needs to be stored and what kind of processing needs to be executed. Typically MongoDB is widely used and you can define the schema (document design) which is tuned for better performance, especially when you are dealing with time series domain.

Node-RED

Node-RED is a tool for wiring together hardware devices, APIs and online services in new and interesting ways. Bluemix provides Node-RED visual editor for creating a flow for your IoT application. For instance, you can create a flow which would listen to messages (topics from IoTF), create rules in JavaScript, execute various other Bluemix services or invoke external services. Every functionality is available as a node and can be dragged in visual editor to create flows by assembling various services and rules for triggering actions. You can even add a custom node to provide custom functionality. This feature is very useful when you want to quickly build a small proof-of-concept (POC) of an IoT application.

You can use the starter template – 'Internet of Things Foundation Starter' in the Bluemix catalog to get started quickly with IoTF and Node-RED. The starter template includes a sample flow that processes temperature readings from a simulated device. Following image shows the Internet of Things Foundation Starter kit in the catalog:

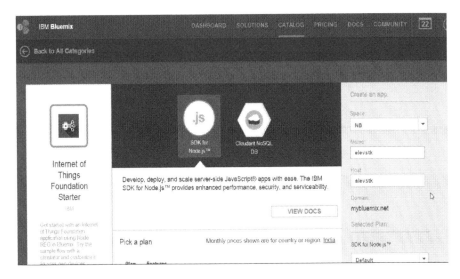

Following image shows the sample Node-RED workflow which receives data from the device through the input connector and throws an alert if the temperature is greater than some value.

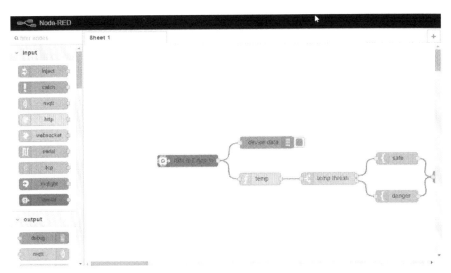

IoT Real-Time Insights

The IoT Real-time Insights is a recent addition to IBM IoT offerings which works in conjunction with IoTF to monitor and contextualize data from devices and apply rules to trigger action. The offering allows you to combine existing master data available from asset management products (like Maximo from IBM) with runtime data from devices for triggering automated action (like an SMS or creating a work order in Maximo). We had discussed the use of asset management and how the data can be leveraged, in the manufacturing use case in Chapter 2.

Note - The problem of integrating asset management solutions, IoT devices, workflow, etc. needs to be looked at holistically starting from how you design a connected product to the realization of end product. In future, we could see a tight end to end integration between asset management products and IoT platforms.

IBM Streaming Analytics

IBM Streaming Analytics service provides analyzing in-flight data in real-time. For those who are familiar with IBM InfoSphere Stream product, the IBM Streaming Analytics is the same technology now available on Bluemix. IBM Streaming Analytics service can analyze millions of events per second and perform analysis with predictable low latency, which is a key requirement for IoT application dealing with millions of connected devices. The service allows you to ingest, analyze and correlate information coming from thousands of real-time sources. In order to build stream applications, you need to download Streams Studio (an eclipse based environment) separately to build streams and deploy via the Streaming Analytics dashboard. IBM Streaming Analytics service is current available in beta and at the time of writing this book, we could not find seamless integration of IBM Streaming Analytics with IoTF. One approach is to use compatible toolkit and adapters (MQTTSource from com.ibm.streamsx.messaging toolkit) in Streams Studio to integrate with IoTF. With this approach, the stream flow gets invoked when message arrives at the MQTT topic defined in IoTF and you can execute the required logic using stream flow components. Once the stream is deployed in Bluemix, you can invoke the stream as part of Node-RED flow or in any application using the Stream REST API.

Note – When we talk about seamless integration in the above context, what we really mean is the ability of components like Streaming Analytics or any components like Apache Spark Streaming to consume data directly from IoTF without the need to build custom adapters or Node-RED flows. We assume this could be simplified through declarative configurations between IoTF and streaming (or any other) components that needs to consume data from IoTF.

Apache Spark and Apache Spark Streaming

Apache Spark is a fast and general purpose engine for big data processing, with built-in modules like streaming, SQL, machine learning and graph processing. Bluemix provides Apache Spark cluster service. The service is currently in beta at the time of writing the book. Apache Spark is used for aggregating and transforming large volumes of data, building analytics solution using Scala and Python, streaming and analyzing data in real-time and even building machine learning models using Spark-MLlib module.

The Apache Spark streaming component provides analyzing streaming data in real-time. This provides one more option for real-time streaming other than IBM Streaming Analytics. The choice of picking up one technology as opposed to other depends on use case requirements, flexibility, maturity of product, availability of skills and various other factors (and in doubt you can reach out to us through the forum at http://enterpriseiotbook.com).

Currently there is no integration provided for Apache Spark streaming service to consume data directly from IoTF, but it could be just a matter of building connectivity adapters and it's a point in time statement. There are alternate options, like storing the data from IoTF into one of the storage database (like ObjectStorage or MongoDB) and apply the Spark programming model. For example, using Python or Scala to create RDD (Resilient Data sources, abstract data model) to aggregate, transform and analyze data. Please note that this is just our approach or one way to integrate Apache Spark service with IoTF. We may see a standard integrated solution in the future.

Machine Learning

IBM provides the predictive analytics service on Bluemix. To build predictive models, you use IBM SPSS Modeler and deploy the model using the administration dashboard of the predictive analytics service. Currently SPSS Modeler is not available with Bluemix, you need to purchase it separately or get an evaluation copy. The IBM SPSS Modeler is used to build and test the predictive model and then the model needs to be exported and deployed as part of predictive analytics service. To access the model at runtime, you can use the REST API from your application (from the Node-RED flow) or web application.

Custom Solutions

These are end to end IoT solutions developed using IoTF and Bluemix services. Apart from the above services, Bluemix provides bunch of other services that can be used for building IoT applications like – Geospatial Analytics to track when devices enter or leave the designated boundaries or mobile push services to send an alert based on the analysis and Embeddable Reporting service to include dashboards in your applications. You can find all the services in the catalog view of Bluemix at https://console.ng.Bluemix.net/catalog/.

As part of IoTF Recipes page, you could also find Application Recipes, which are end to end examples that can be used as a starting point for building IoT applications. The example application recipes include machine condition monitoring, geo-spatial analysis, track and trace, real-time dashboards for wearable and many more. These application recipes use IoTF and various Bluemix services and are contributed by IBM and the open source community.

Implementation Overview

Let's design the connected elevator solution we discussed in the second chapter using IBM IoT stack.

Note – You could easily realize the connected car solution that we discussed earlier in Microsoft IoT implementation with IBM IoT implementation. If you have followed the description of the services provided by Microsoft and IBM closely, it is more or less the same. Taking reference of the Microsoft implementation, all you have to do is replace Microsoft IoT components with its IBM equivalent. A comparison chart of services offered by various IoT cloud platforms is provided at the end of this chapter.

Hardware and Connectivity

In this section we would discuss the hardware and connectivity approach for the elevator use case. The elevator manufacturer has already invested in Maximo (IBM Asset Management solution) for managing the physical assets and workflows and now wants to start the journey towards a smarter connected solution. We described the set of phases in the second chapter and how can a manufacturer use each of these phases to incrementally implement an IoT solution. We will realize the elevator use case using IBM IoT stack through the following phases viz. monitoring (which includes asset management), condition maintenance and finally predictive maintenance.

We would not go into the details of each phase again, but only talk about the implementation steps. The manufacturer as part of a connected design adds various new sensors to the existing elevator control unit. The elevator manufacturer as a first step, leverages its existing investment and tries to keep the connectivity and communication protocol between elevator control unit and rest of components same and builds up the device connectivity code using the IoTF Embedded C Device library and converts the non-proprietary protocols to MQTT and deploys it in the elevator control unit. The elevator control unit device is provisioned with secure access as part of the device registration process using IoTF dashboard (or IoTF APIs).

The control unit can be thought of as a gateway which connects to IoTF and do local processing and conversion. It collates the data from various sensors and maintains the communication and wraps the sensor data into JSON data and sends it over MQTT protocol to IoTF platform.

Software Implementation Overview

Following are the high level steps that needs to be performed in Bluemix

1. Create IoTF service
2. Register devices and get access credentials
3. Provision devices (elevator control device)
4. Create storage (database for storing raw data from devices, asset mapping)
5. Create Node-RED flow   (end to end execution flow)
6. Create Push Notification Service (mobile notifications)
7. Create ML model (anomaly and predictive maintenance)

The above step is just one of the approaches to building end to end IoT application. Instead of Node-RED flow we could also use IBM Streaming Analytics or Apache Spark service. As mentioned earlier, the service is currently in beta and does not have seamless integration with IoTF. As part of the solution, we can create separate Node-RED flows as it's easier to maintain and replace the flow by Streaming Analytics services for high throughput cases where complex requirements like correlating and working with multiple data sources is required.

Following shows the connected elevator solution using IoTF and Bluemix services.

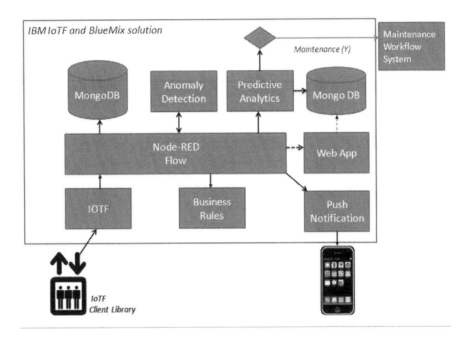

The IoTF service receives the data from the connected elevator over MQTT protocol. A Node-RED flow is created which receives the connected elevator device data from the corresponding topic. To map the runtime data from devices to physical asset in Maximo, a database (MongoDB) is used to store the mapping.

We create multiple Node-RED flows as shown below, they all listen to events from specified MQTT topic.

- A Node-RED flow stores the data in MongoDB
- A set of Node-RED flows works on data directly and evaluates the required monitoring and condition-based rules.

- A Node-RED flow for predictive maintenance which creates the abstract data model and calls the predictive analytics service via the REST API
- A NODE RED flow for anomaly detection. Note this is bidirectional in the implementation diagram above, as the response from anomaly is send to the mobile operator using push notification.
- Based on the outcome, the required action item is executed by the above flows (SMS via the push service or invoking a work order in Maximo through REST call).

We have not covered the details of building the predictive model as it was already discussed as part Microsoft IoT solution. The approach of building a machine model, whether using Microsoft or IBM tools or open source options remains the same. You build the model and train the model iteratively using the raw data from the connected devices, asset metadata and historical maintenance records. The real challenge in building the model is choosing the right features, cleansing and aggregating the data, applying algorithms, training the model and continuously iterating it to reasonably predict outcome.

We use the SPSS Modeler which provides the capabilities to prepare the data and build models, similar to Azure ML that we discussed earlier. We use the SPSS Modeler to build predictive models and detect anomaly.

Once the model is developed, it is deployed in Bluemix through the predictive maintenance dashboard and can be accessed through the Node-RED flow through the HTTP/REST API connector node. This completes the connected elevator implementation using IBM IoTF and Bluemix.

Building application with Amazon IoT Platform

In this chapter, we would look at how to realize the IoT use case using Amazon Web Services (AWS). Similar to Microsoft Azure and IBM Bluemix, AWS offers a host of services to enable creating IoT applications.

Amazon recently (on 8th October 2015) announced the AWS IoT (currently in beta) service at their AWS re:Invent event. AWS IoT makes it easier to build IoT applications. AWS IoT platform allows you to collect, store, analyze and take actions against large volumes of data streaming from your connected devices.

This was an important update from Amazon as prior to this announcement, there were no direct IoT offering from Amazon like the IoT Hub from Microsoft or IBM IoTF. However this did not stop anyone from building an IoT application on AWS, as you could develop custom application or host open source components (like Mosquito for MQTT) which provides similar functionality on AWS. With the acquisition of 21emetry (and its ThingFabric IoT platform) in March 2015, we feel they had closed this gap earlier, but there were no official announcement on how ThingFabric capabilities would be used in context of AWS. We assume they leveraged the ThingFabric platform (MQTT and HTTP support) and the rules integration from ThingFabric which allows connecting to various AWS services. Please note this is purely our view point and there is no official confirmation on how ThingFabric platform is leveraged (if at all) internally with the latest Amazon IoT beta product.

Note - We had built an IoT Stack using AWS and ThingFabric prior to the recent AWS IoT announcement. If you are interested in details, please reach out to us via the book forum at http://enterpriseiotbook.com/. Please note AWS IoT is the way forward for building IoT applications on AWS stack. We updated this section prior to releasing the book, to include the latest updates on the Amazon IoT service.

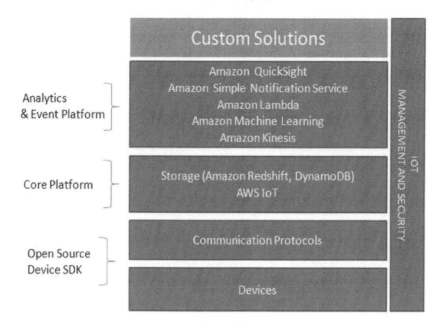

IoT Stack Mapping for Amazon IoT

Let's analyze all the components –

AWS IoT Device SDK

AWS IoT Device SDK simplifies the process of connecting devices securely to the AWS IoT platform over MQTT protocol. The device SDKs currently supports C SDK for Linux, libraries for Arduino platform and Node.JS libraries for embedded platforms like BeagleBone, Raspberry Pi etc.

All bi directional communication between devices and AWS IoT platform is encrypted through Transport Layer Security (TLS) protocol. We would talk about the security aspects in the later section. The device SDK also allows an option of using third party cryptographic libraries and TLS 1.2 certificates for connecting devices to the AWS IoT platform securely.

Tip - The AWS IoT Starter Kits provides everything you need in a box to get started with Amazon IoT platform. Just plug and play the device and it is connected to AWS IoT platform. You can purchase the kits from Amazon.com.

AWS IoT

AWS IoT is a highly scalable and managed cloud platform that allows devices to securely connect and interact with AWS services and other devices over standardized MQTT and HTTP protocol. AWS IoT also allows applications to interact with devices even when they are offline by storing their latest state and later syncing the state back to actual devices when they are connected back.

The AWS IoT platform consists of core set of capabilities as shown in the figure below. This includes a device gateway, device registry, rules engine and device shadows component.

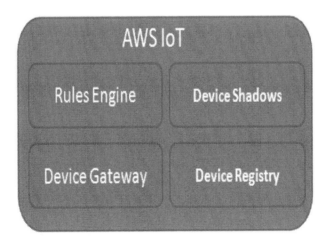

Let's understand each of the components –

- Device Gateway: The AWS IoT Device Gateway is a highly scalable managed service that enables devices to securely communicate with AWS IoT. The Device Gateway supports publish subscribe model and provides support for MQTT and HTTP 1.1 protocols. We had discussed the pub-sub pattern earlier in our Chapter 1. The main advantage of using this pattern is that it decouples sender and consumer thereby allowing new devices to get connected and start receiving the messages by subscribing to relevant topics.

- Device Registry: Device Registry stores the metadata about the devices and act as identity store of devices. Each device is assigned a unique identity by Device registry during registration. We had described the typical features of device registry earlier in Chapter 1.

- Device Shadows: Device Shadows is a unique capability provided as part of the AWS IoT platform which creates a virtual device or shadow of the device that contains its latest state. Application can communicate with shadow/virtual device through the APIs even if the actual physical device is offline. When the actual device gets connected, AWS IoT automatically synchronizes the state and pushes changes to the actual device based on changes that was done on the virtual device.

- Rules Engine: Rules engine is a highly scalable engine that transforms and route incoming messages from devices to AWS services based on business rules you have authored. Rules are authored using SQL like syntax and query is made against a MQTT Topic to extract the required data from the incoming message. The incoming message needs to be in JSON format. Here is a sample query

```
SELECT *FROM 'iot/ccar-ad/#'WHERE speed >120
```

In above query, "iot/ccar-ad/#' is the topic where devices publish the following JSON message. In this case the rule would be evaluated to true as speed is 140 km/hour.

```
{
"deviceid":"audi22",
```

```
"speed":140,
"gps":{
"latitude":...,
"longitude":...
}
"tyre1":30,
.....
}
```

AWS IoT also provides various options for secure communication between devices and the AWS IoT platform. Understanding the end to end security strategy for your IoT application is a key step, as it includes devices, AWS IoT platform and rest of AWS services being used as part of the IoT application. Let's talk about it in detail in the next section.

Device Security, Authorization and Authentication

Let's understand how devices can securely connect to AWS IoT platform and process of authorizing devices. AWS IoT platform provides secure, bi-directional communication between devices and the AWS cloud. Devices connect using choice of identity through one of the 3 options – Digital certificates (X.509 certificate), AWS authentication through user and passwords or leveraging their own identity provider or third party providers like Google, Facebook using Amazon Cognito. Based on identity choice, you choose which application protocol to be used for communication and how you want to manage identities. For instance, you would typically choose X.509 certificate with MQTT protocol as it would allow bi directional communication between devices and AWS IoT platform to be encrypted. Amazon Cognito is used if you have already invested in third party identity management and want to leverage it for IoT applications and HTTP protocol for managing identities using AWS Identity and Access Management (IAM) service. We would not recommend using HTTP protocol for devices unless a MQTT library doesn't exist for that device.

Note - TLS requires digital certificates for authentication. AWS supports X.509 certificates that enable asymmetric keys to be used with devices. AWS IoT command line interface (CLI) makes it easier to create, manage and deploy X.509 digital certificates.

Once a device is authenticated, authorization is handled through policies. Policies lets you execute device operations (connect, publish, subscribe, receive) based on the permissions defined. You create policies based on your identity choices, for instance you create AWS IoT polices and attach it for X.509 certificate and Amazon Cognito, for IAM user management you create IAM policies through the IAM console. Once authorized, the specific operations can be performed. This completes the device communication with the AWS IoT platform. Now your IoT application would like to invoke other AWS services, like persisting the device data from topic to DynamoDB or processing large volumes of data streams in real-time through Amazon Kinesis stream instance. This is handled through the rules instance as discussed earlier. In order to access the particular Amazon Kinesis stream instance, you need to have a policy defined in IAM, which is used by the rule instance to allow AWS IoT to access the Amazon Kinesis stream instance securely. This ensures an end to end secure connectivity between devices and Amazon IoT platform and from Amazon IoT platform to rest of AWS services.

The following diagram shows an execution flow for a secured MQTT connectivity between devices and AWS IoT platform.

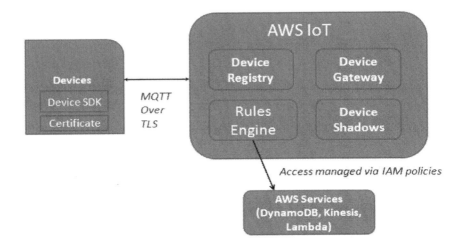

To summarize an execution flow for a secured MQTT connectivity, the onus is on you to assign unique identities to each device through Device Registry, create and manage certificates on the devices and connect to Amazon IoT over TLS protocol using these certificates. You can use Amazon Device SDK which provides libraries for TLS based authentication. Once devices establishes a connection, the Amazon IoT platform in turn is responsible for authenticating your devices based on the client X.509 certificate, validating it based on public keys. Once authenticated, authorization of operations happens based on the policies defined in certificate and valid operations are executed. For instance a device may only be able to read messages from a topic and not publish on the topic. As discussed earlier, to interact with other AWS services, you author rules and define how you want to route the messages. For instance, you can route the messages to Amazon Kinesis for processing large volumes of data streams in real-time. In order to access the particular Amazon Kinesis stream instance, you need to have policy (roles and permissions) defined in IAM, and your rule instance uses the policy to allow AWS IoT to access the Amazon Kinesis stream instance securely.

Storage

AWS provides various options for storage - Amazon DynamoDB (NoSQL database), Amazon Redshift or Amazon Relation Database service. For IoT applications, the initial choice is to use Amazon DynamoDB. Amazon DynamoDB is a highly scalable, high performance NoSQL database with single-digit millisecond latency at any scale. It is a fully managed database service and provides first class support to trigger events based on data modifications in tables via Amazon Lambda service. We would talk about Amazon Lambda service in later section.

Amazon Redshift on the another hand, is a fast, fully managed, petabyte-scale data warehouse that delivers fast query by parallelizing queries across nodes to analyze massive volumes of data. Depending on the volume of data that needs to be analyzed over a period of time and complexity of analytics queries, you can move over to Amazon Redshift or import the data from DynamoDB to Redshift. You need to have the right schema design with Amazon Redshift as it would impact querying, indexing and performance of your queries. For instance, if you need to find out average power consumption of a connected city based on each location at runtime, you are dealing with at least millions of records. In such scenario, Amazon Redshift may be an ideal choice. Also, not all device data needs to be treated equally and stored in Redshift, but only a set of key actionable data sets, streaming from millions of connected devices, which are used to derive actionable insights by running complex analytics queries on it.

From an integration perspective, you can directly store the data from devices into DynamoDB using Amazon IoT rules engine. You need to author rules in Amazon IoT to trigger on specified MQTT topic, select the message and also provide the IAM role which has access to DynamoDB service and can perform required operations (like insert) on DynamoDB. Following shows an example of a rule which dumps all device data from topic 'ccar' into DynamoDB table 'ccardb':

```
{
"sql":"SELECT * FROM 'topic/ccar'",
"ruleDisabled":false,
"actions":[{
"dynamoDB":{
```

```
"tableName":"ccardb",
"hashKeyField":"key",
"hashKeyValue":'${topic(3)}',
"rangeKeyField":"timestamp",
"rangeKeyValue":'${timestamp()}',
"roleArn":"arn:aws:iam::1xxx/iot-actions-role"
}
}]
}
```

The above assumes you have created a DynamoDB table with name as
ccardb. As part of table name creation, you specify the primary key
attributes as Hash and Range or Hash. Choosing the right Hash and Range
is a key consideration as this would impact how the data is indexed and
retrieved. In the above case, we choose topic name and timestamp as
hash and range values.

We talked about the time series domain earlier, you can design the
DynamoDB schema in a way that it can handle time series operations
effectively.

To store the incoming data into Amazon Redshift, you can use Amazon
Kinesis Firehose. We will talk about Amazon Kinesis Firehose in the next
section. You specify the Amazon Kinesis stream instance name and IAM
role for access. The stream is configured to dump the data into Amazon
Redshift.

Following shows an example:

```
{
"sql":"SELECT * FROM 'topic/ccar'",
"ruleDisabled":false,
"actions":[{
" firehose":{
"roleArn":" arn:aws:iam::2xxx/iot-actions-role ",
"deliveryStreamName":"ccarfst"
}
}]
}
```

Amazon Kinesis

Amazon Kinesis platform provides real-time data processing, enabling applications to capture continuous stream of data from devices and other sources, analyze it at runtime to generate real-time dashboards or trigger required action. Amazon Kinesis platform consists of three services:

- Amazon Kinesis Firehose: Amazon Kinesis Firehose lets you capture streaming data and store the data directly into Amazon S3 and Amazon Redshift and make it available in near real-time for reporting and analysis.

- Amazon Kinesis Streams: Amazon Kinesis stream lets you build custom real-time highly scalable streaming applications based on your requirements, such as real-time optimizations from multi stage process flows. Let's take an example of a connected airport and one of the use cases is around providing fastest journey time for passengers throughout the airport. The process would involve streaming data from multiple connected sources and points of interest , like check-in counter, security gates, existing passenger movements, baggage handling and services, immigrations etc. and coming up with specialized set of algorithms that could correlate the data at real-time and predict passenger journey time and then optimize it.

- Amazon Kinesis Analytics: Amazon Kinesis Analytics service (currently not released at time of writing this book) will make it easier to extract and analyze data using SQL like queries and send the output of queries to specified services (like AWS Lambda) to create alerts and take correction action in real-time. Prior to Amazon Kinesis Analytics service, you need to create your own custom AWS Lambda functions to extract the data. The incoming data is usually in JSON format and your custom functions would use the JSON APIs to extract the data and execute custom rules and take action based on the outcome.

You can directly stream the data from devices into Amazon Kinesis Firehose or Amazon Kinesis Streams using Amazon IoT rules engine.

You need to author rules to trigger on specified MQTT topic, select the message and also provide the IAM role which has access the Kinesis instance. Following is configuration that needs to be set for accessing the Kinesis streaming instance:

```
"kinesis":{
"roleArn":"string",//IAM Role
"streamName":"string",// Kinesis stream instance name
"partitionKey":"string"// Kinesis stream partition key
},
```

Following is the configuration for Amazon Kinesis Firehose:

```
"firehose":{
"roleArn":"string",//IAM Role
"deliveryStreamName":"string"// Stream name
}
```

You can also use Amazon Kinesis Client Library to build required applications (like real-time dashboards) which can consume the stream data in real-time or emit data to other AWS services like Amazon Lambda for event processing.

Note - Amazon Kinesis Aggregators is a Java framework that enables the automatic creation of real-time aggregated time series data from Amazon Kinesis streams. The project is available at https://github.com/awslabs/amazon-kinesis-aggregators and provides a good start on how to provide time series analysis on the incoming data.

Amazon ML

AWS provides Amazon Machine Learning service which provides end-to-end support and tooling for creating, training and fine-tuning machine learning models directly from supported data sources (Amazon Redshift, Amazon S3 or Amazon RDS), along with deployment and monitoring. The models can be executed through APIs as part of your process to obtain predictions for your applications.

Amazon ML provides interactive visual tools to create, evaluate, and deploy machine learning models. Amazon ML also provides the implementation of common data transformations which is extremely helpful to prepare the data for evaluation.

Amazon Machine Learning service is based on the same proven, highly scalable, ML technology used by Amazon to perform critical functions like supply chain management and fraudulent transaction identification. You could see various machine learning algorithms (like classification, recommendation etc.) in action on Amazon website.

AWS Lambda

AWS Lambda allows you to run your custom code in AWS cloud. You need to supply the code as Node.js (or Java) function and create a deployment package with the required dependency. As mentioned earlier, AWS Lambda functions can be executed asynchronously based on events from other AWS services like Amazon Kinesis. You can specify this mapping from AWS Lambda console, to associate your Lambda function with Amazon Kinesis source name. AWS Lambda functions are a great way to invoke external services (like invoking a REST call for workflow generation in a SAP system), sending alerts and notifications on mobiles through Amazon Simple Notification Service or any custom code that needs to be executed based on the desired condition.

Apart from the above services, AWS provides bunch of other services that can be used as part of the IoT applications like – Amazon ElastiCache for in-memory cache for storing asset meta data or using AWS CloudHSM service providing hardware appliance based secured key storage for handling sensitive data on cloud, for instance dealing with data from health care devices as per regulatory compliance. You can find all services at the products page at https://aws.amazon.com/products/

Implementation Overview

The strategy for building the IoT application on AWS is pretty much the same as discussed earlier for IBM and Microsoft IoT offerings. You build IoT applications by composing the relevant AWS services and AWS IoT services. For instance, you could replace the Microsoft Azure services with services being offered by AWS for the connected car solution that we went through earlier. At the end of this chapter, we have provided a comparison chart of services offered by various IoT cloud platforms.

To summarize for the connected car solution, we went through three phases of implementation – real-time flow, offline/batch phase where we developed machine learning models and finally the third phase where we modified our real-time flow to integrate the machine learning model. We would not go over the entire steps in detail but summarize the integration below. Kindly refer to Microsoft IoT implementation section for details on how we arrived at the final (the third) step of the solution.

Given below is the final step of the connected car solution using Amazon IoT.

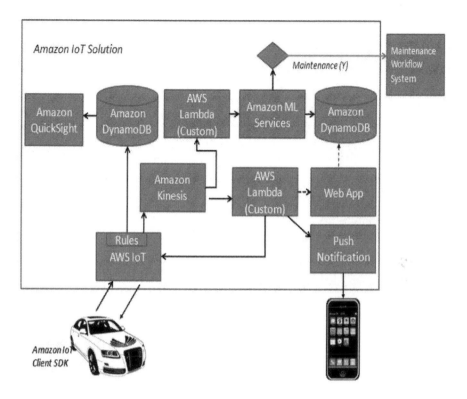

Amazon IoT Solution — Maintenance (Y) — Maintenance Workflow System — Amazon QuickSight — Amazon DynamoDB — AWS Lambda (Custom) — Amazon ML Services — Amazon DynamoDB — Amazon Kinesis — AWS Lambda (Custom) — Web App — Rules AWS IoT — Push Notification — *Amazon IoT Client SDK*

Hardware and Connectivity

For connecting the hardware device to the Amazon IoT platform, we use AWS IoT Device SDKs. We use MQTT protocol over TLS for secure communication. We went through the details earlier in Device Security, Authorization and Authentication section.   We need to register the device in registry, create certificates, assign policies and use the relevant SDKs. The following are the high level steps

1.   Create Thing in Device Registry
2.   Create Certificates and Policies for secured communication
3.   Attach Certificate to Thing
4.   Generate SDKs

For the above steps, you can use AWS IoT Web console or AWS CLI (command line interface) commands. As part of device provision step, manufacturers would typically use AWS CLI as that would provide an ability to automate the process and use their own private key to generate certificates using AWS command.

We use the web console and list down the AWS CLI specific commands for reference.

- Create a new Thing by selecting the Create Thing button from the create panel view. Give some logical name to your thing which closely resembles your device. You will associate an actual device to this Thing later. Thing represents a virtual device and you can perform any operations on it, similar to an actual device. We really liked this feature as it helped us to create an end application without even integrating a physical device.

The AWS CLI command for creating a Thing is:

```
>>aws iot create-thing --thing-name "ccar-dev-
mh2279"
```

Please note you need to have the right policies to invoke the create-thing command. By default, root user has all the rights. If you create a new user, make sure he has the right policies to execute various AWS

IoT commands. Attach is a sample policy document which allows most of the administrative IoT commands and can be used to create a new policy. Once the policy is created, you can assign it to the required users through IAM console.

```
{
"Version":"2012-10-17",
"Statement":[
{
"Effect":"Allow",
"Action":[
"iot:CreateKeysAndCertificate",
"iot:DescribeCertificate",
"iot:AttachPrincipalPolicy",
"iot:CreateThing",
"iot:list-things",
"iot:CreatePolicy",
"iot:AttachThingPrincipal",
"iot:DescribeEndpoint"
],
"Resource":"*"
}
]
}
```

- On the next screen, you can click on View Thing option to view the details about the Thing as shown below.

AWS IoT

Your new thing has been created. Click 'View thing' to continue.

From there, you can connect a device to this thing, or add a rule to take actions when your thing publishes a message.

View thing

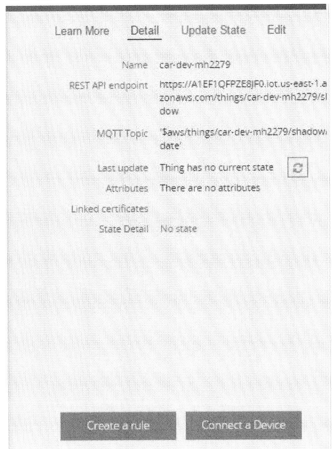

Learn More   Detail   Update State   Edit

Name	car-dev-mh2279
REST API endpoint	https://A1EF1QFPZE8JF0.iot.us-east-1.a zonaws.com/things/car-dev-mh2279/sh dow
MQTT Topic	'$aws/things/car-dev-mh2279/shadow/ date'
Last update	Thing has no current state
Attributes	There are no attributes
Linked certificates	
State Detail	No state

Create a rule   Connect a Device

114

- Next, we need to create certificates and policies. One option is to select the Create a Certificate and Create a Policy from create panel view. The other option is to quickly generate all the steps using the Connect a Device option. This would generate certificates, policies, attach the policy to certificates, attach certificate to Thing and also provide secret key and public key. Click on "Connect a Device" in the Detail view of Thing.

- Select an SDK based on the programming model supported by your device. We choose Node.js as we can test the integration easily from any available environment's (laptops, phones, etc.) which supports Node.js runtime. Click on Generate Certificate and Policy

Connect a Device

Connect your device to one of our many supported SDKs.

○ Embedded C   ◉ NodeJS
○ Arduino Yun

First, you will need to create and download security credentials for your device. The following steps will help you to create and download security credentials (a certificate for authentication, and a policy that defines what the device using this certificate is allowed to do).

You can generate a certificate with 1-click. When you generate a certificate, we will also generate a default security policy named car-dev-mh2279-Policy. You can modify this security policy at any time through the 'Resources' panel of this console.

Generate Certificate and Policy

If you are using AWS CLI command, you need to use the AWS IoT *create-keys-and-certificate* command for creating certificate and keys, AWS IoT *create-policy* command for creating policy and for attaching policy to certificate you need to use AWS IoT *attach-principal-policy* command. Following shows the snapshots of the commands.

```
c:\ccar>aws iot create-policy --policy-name "PubSubConnect" --policy-document fi
le://c:/ccar/pubsub.policy
{
    "policyName": "PubSubConnect",
    "policyArn": "arn:aws:iot:us-east-1:349094522135:policy/PubSubConnect",
    "policyDocument": "{\n    \"Version\": \"2012-10-17\", \n    \"Statement\":
[\n\t{\n        \"Effect\": \"Allow\",\n            \"Action\":[\"iot:Publish\",\"io
t:Subscribe\",\"iot:Connect\"],\n            \"Resource\": [\"arn:aws:iot:us-east-1:
349094522135:thing/ccar-dev-mh02711\"]\n    }\n\t]\n}",
    "policyVersionId": "1"
}
c:\ccar>aws iot attach-principal-policy --principal "arn:aws:iot:us-east-1:34909
```

- In the next screen, download the public key, private key and certificate. Click Confirm.

Please download these files and save them in a safe place. Certificates can be retrieved at any time, but the Private and Public Keys will not be retrievable after closing this form.

- Download Public Key
- Download Private Key
- Download Certificate

Confirm & Start Connecting

- In the AWS IoT Node.js SDK screen, copy the generated code values as we would need this for connecting our Thing to AWS IoT platform. Click on Return to Thing detail.

AWS IoT Node.js SDK

Download the AWS IoT Node.js SDK.

Set up the SDK using the instructions in our README on GitHub.

Add in the following sample code based on your account, Thing, and new certificate:

```
{
    "host": "A                                    ",
    "port": 8883,
    "clientId": "car-dev-mh2279",
    "thingName": "car-dev-mh2279",
    "caCert": "root-CA.crt",
    "clientCert": "                            t",
    "privateKey": "f                           "
}
```

Start one of the sample applications found in the SDK. You can use the AWS IoT console to observe the state of your Thing's Shadow and interact with your device by updating the Shadow.

Return to Thing Detail

- In the console, you would see the certificate and policy created. The policy document name would be typically <thingname>-Policy. Click on it and you would see the policy document. The generated policy document grants all IoT operations to all resources, you can change this at runtime, by allowing only specific operations like publish or subscribe. This provides an ability to revoke or grant access to devices connecting the IoT platform without even touching the device.

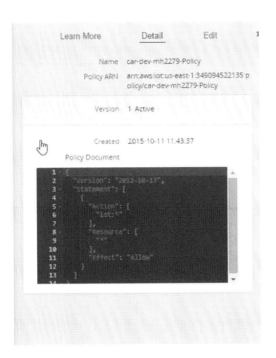

- Now click on the certificate (which would have the longest name) and you would see the certificate attached to the Thing and to the policy document that was created. This completes one configuration. We would now communicate with the IoT platform with the generated artefacts.

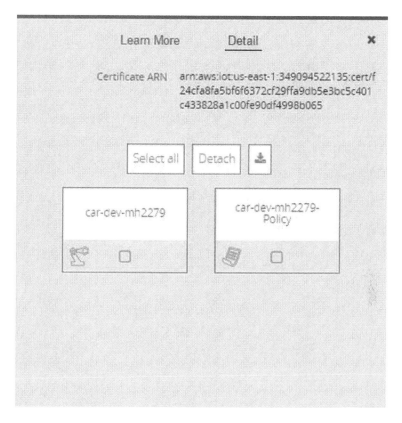

We would use Node.js for testing the secure connectivity with the IoT platform and send/receive messages. The following steps assume that you have Node.js runtime installed.

- Install the Amazon IoT Device SDK by the following command

```
npm install aws-iot-device-sdk
```

- Once installed, create a Node.js sample which would use the installed aws-iot-device-sdk module. There are lot of samples provided in examples directory of AWS IoT device SDK installation. Given below is sample Node.js file for testing. Save it as CCARTest.js. Replace host, clientId, thingName, caPath, cerPath, keyPath and region value below based on your environment value. You would have received the value for your environment after the certificate was generated. For caPath certificate, download the root CA certificate which acts as a trusted

source from Verisign forthis location -
https://www.symantec.com/content/en/us/enterprise/verisign/roots
/VeriSign-Class%203-Public-Primary-Certification-Authority-G5.pem
and save as root-CA.cert

```
var awsIot = require('aws-iot-device-sdk');

var device = awsIot.device({
    host:"xx.iot.us-east-1.amazonaws.com",
    port:8883,
    clientId:"car-dev-mh2279",
    thingName:"car-dev-mh2279",
    caPath:"root-CA.crt",
    certPath:"f42cec7751-certificate.pem.crt",
    keyPath:"f42cec7751-private.pem.key",
    region:"us-east-1"
});

device
.on('connect',function(){
    console.log('connect');
//subscribe..
    device.subscribe('topic/ccar');
//publish..
    device.publish('topic/ccar', JSON.stringify({
speed:80}));
});

device
.on('message',function(topic, payload){
    console.log('message received - ', topic,
payload.toString());
});

device
.on('error',function(error){
    console.log('error', error);
});
```

---

*Note - At the time of writing the book, the aws-iot-device-sdk Node.js
library has a small bug. Open awt-iot-device-sdk\index.js and wrap the*

device and thing in require tag in single quotes as shown below. This has been reported via - https://github.com/aws/aws-iot-device-sdk-js/issues/5

```
module.exports.device = require('./device');
module.exports.thingShadow = require('./thing');
```

The above code imports the 'aws-iot-device-sdk' module, creates a device configuration by passing in the required parameters – certificates, private-key and other parameters values as shown above. The configuration is used to create a secure connection over TLS to the Amazon IoT platform. As you recollect, we had attached the certificate to our Thing and policy in Amazon IoT. Based on the thingName, the Amazon IoT retrieves the certificates and authenticates using private and public key combination and once authenticated, it authorizes operations based on the policy document attached to the certificate. Once the device is connected, the connect call back method in our code is invoked. For testing, our code acts as a publisher as well as subscriber. In the connect method, we first subscribe to topic named 'topic/ccar' and then publish a sample JSON request to 'topic/ccar'. In a real world, the JSON data would be an actual vehicle data from the connected car. The call back method is invoked whenever a message is received on the topic – topic/ccar. Our code simply displays the value in the console.

- Next run the above CCARTest.js file using the command node CCARTest.js. You would see the following output as shown below.

```
C:\ccar>node CCARTest.js
connect
message received  -  topic/ccar {"speed":80}
^C
C:\ccar>
```

We are done connecting a virtual device to Amazon IoT platform securely and even tested out sending and receiving a message from Amazon IoT platform. Once the message reaches the Amazon IoT platform, we next look at how to build applications by composing the various AWS services.

Software Implementation Overview

The first step is to understand how you want to process the incoming data based on your requirements and what AWS services you would use to build your IoT applications. You then create rules using the rules engine which would route incoming data to one or multiple AWS services to process the data.

For our connected car application, we create two rules, one rules route's the message to a Kinesis Stream instance and other rule directly inserts the incoming data to Amazon DynamoDB tables. We discussed the rule configuration in Storage section earlier.

For real-time dashboards and visualization, we plan to use Amazon QuickSight. Amazon QuickSight is currently under preview and integration looks promising. Amazon QuickSight integrates seamlessly with DynamoDB and other AWS services, so it would be easier to pull the relevant schema and build visualizations quickly. We would update this section with latest updates once we get access to QuickSight. If you are planning to build your own reporting, we suggest you to hold on and try out the QuickSight once available. This looks similar to PowerBI from Microsoft which we had discussed earlier.

Before we talk about Kinesis stream instance, we will look at how Machine Learning models are developed using Amazon ML for the connected car use case. The approach and step required to build predictive models is exactly the same as mentioned in Building the Machine Learning Model section as part of the Microsoft IoT Stack. Instead of using Azure ML we use Amazon ML and we choose to build machine learning models iteratively using offline process. Amazon ML as discussed earlier provides interactive visual tools to create, evaluate, and deploy machine learning models. Amazon ML provides implementation of common data transformations which is extremely helpful to prepare the data. As part of the prepare data phase, you load the data. Our raw data from connected car is stored in Amazon DynamoDB. Currently AWS ML tool does not support directly importing the data from Amazon DynamoDB. It currently supports Amazon Redshift, Amazon S3 and Amazon RDS (MYSQL only) only. So you need to make the data available in S3 via CSV format or import the data into Redshift. For the connected car use case, we develop two machine learning models (as discussed earlier) – regression model for predictive maintenance and multi-class classification for driver behaviour analysis.

Once the Amazon ML is developed, it can be consumed through the Amazon ML API. The AWS ML APIs is available at http://docs.aws.amazon.com/machine-learning/latest/APIReference/API_Predict.html. The integration diagram described earlier in the Implementation Overview section shows how predictive maintenance is included in the final step. The integration of driver behaviour analysis is pretty much the same and in this case the output goes to mobile and web instead of a maintenance request.

Coming back to Kinesis stream instance, we use it for processing the continuous flow of data from devices in real-time. Multiple applications can receive the streams of data and work in parallel. For the connected car use case, we emit the data from the Amazon Kinesis stream instance to 2 AWS Lambda components. One AWS Lambda component invokes the machine learning models using the APIs and based on the outcome (if maintenance is required), invokes the external maintenance system through a secured REST call for repairing of the equipment.

The second AWS Lambda component executes the rule conditions (i.e. driving speed > 100 km/hour, geo-fencing conditions). If the conditions are met, a notification is sent to the registered mobile via the push notification service. This completes one end to end integration flow.

The Kinesis stream instance acts as the data stream processing backbone, allowing new integration logic to be added to existing flow by simply integrating with Kinesis stream instance. We talked about many use cases in Chapter 2 for connected car, like driver assistance, recommendations based on driving patterns, usage-based insurance, etc. and each can be realized using separate AWS Lambda components or AWS services.

Building Application with GE Predix IoT Platform

In this section, we would look at how to realize the IoT use case using Predix Cloud platform. As quoted from the Predix website – "Predix brings together GE's legacy of industrial domain expertise with our deep investments in cutting-edge technology and data science. The result? An industrial cloud platform (PaaS) that helps you build connectivity into your Industrial Internet strategy – across all verticals."

Predix platform is targeted towards creating Industrial Internet applications. The Predix platform provides out of the box support for industry protocols like Modbus, DDS and OPC-UA which makes it easier to integrate with existing industrial devices, along with a dedicated software stack "Predix Machine" which can be run on edge devices or machine controllers (in manufacturing plants) to do local analytics.

 The Predix platform is built on open source CloudFoundry platform and provides a catalog of services to develop, compose and deploy Industrial internet applications.

Note - From a strategy perspective, whether it's IBM, Amazon, Microsoft or Predix platform, all provides a scalable cloud platform (PaaS), development tools and set of services (analytics, real-time streaming, databases, reporting etc) and device SDKs targeted towards building IoT applications. All of these big players are building an ecosystem of partners from working with Original Equipment Manufacturer (OEM) to embed their device stack, or partnering with system integrators, independent software vendors, start-ups and development communities to enable them quickly to build internet of thing applications.

In the first chapter, we had discussed about a generic Enterprise IoT stack. The following shows our representation on how the Predix IoT services can be mapped to our generic Enterprise IoT stack.

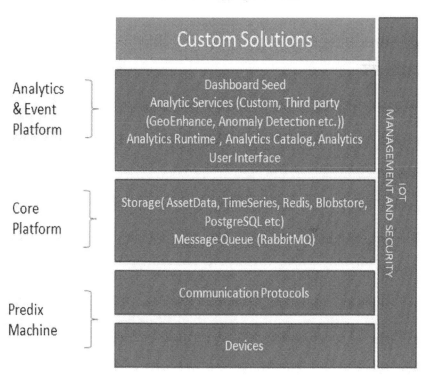

IoT Stack Mapping for Predix

Let's go through the components in details.

Predix Machine

Predix Machine is a software stack component that can run on any class of devices (supporting Java runtime) or installed on a device gateway and provide connectivity to the Predix Cloud platform. We had talked about smart gateway in Chapter 1 which provides local analytical and filtering support at the edge of devices. The Predix Machine is an example of a smart gateway providing analytical and operational services at the edge, along with secured bidirectional connectivity to industrial devices. Predix Machine can integrate with existing industrial devices through its in-built support for protocols like Modbus, OPC-UA, MQTT or TCP and then transmit the required data of interest from these industrial devices to the Predix Cloud. For connectivity to Predix cloud, Predix Machine provides support for secured HTTPS, MQTT and WebSocket protocol. Essentially, existing industrial devices can easily be connected to cloud for data collection, analytics and remote monitoring.

Tip – Using other cloud platforms or solutions, you can still connect to Industrial devices. There are alternatives like using the Modbus Driver i.e. http://eclipse.github.io/kura/doc/kura-modbus-driver.html or building your own adapter and integrating it with your IoT Stack.

Predix software stack is developed using Java/OSGI framework and provides an OSGI based container for running applications and services. Using the Predix Machine Software SDK, you can customize the OSGI container to generate the container code for only the required features. For instance, you can skip generation of "Predix Machine Store and Forward" feature if you don't require local processing on devices. If you are deploying the Predix Machine to a gateway device you would need most of the feature set and while deploying it on the sensor nodes you would need to cut down the feature set to bare minimum. The documentation at https://www.predix.io/docs/ (https://www.predix.io/docs/#MgHwD2pM) provides clear guidelines on the feature set, memory requirements and footprint for each of these features and a list of verified platforms where Predix Machine was successfully installed and executed.

For management of devices, the Predix EdgeManager service is provided. The EdgeManager provides a single interface for monitoring devices, configuring security and carrying out various device management functionalities.

Core Platform

The core platform comprises of messaging and storage services. The messaging middleware service is offered by RabbitMQ (by Pivotal). Essentially this is scalable secured RabbitMQ installation managed by the Predix Cloud. The messaging middleware service as described in Chapter 1 – IoT Messaging Middleware section provides scalable, highly available and persistent reliable messaging between devices and various cloud services. RabbitMQ by default supports the AMQP protocol. RabbitMQ also supports MQTT protocol and programming APIs like Java, .NET and Erlang.

From a storage service perspective, Predix provides choice of Time Series service for handling time series data, SQL Database (PostgreSQL) for SQL based interactions, a high performance Key-Value store database and a Blobstore for handling very large object storages (like medical images which spans in GBs). The choice of using one storage service as opposed to others depends on the application requirements. We had discussed the requirements earlier during the course of chapter. The storage services are in-line with rest of the cloud providers.

Predix also provides an Asset Data service to enable creating asset model that describes the logical structure and relationships between the assets and create instances of the asset model. You can design the asset model based on your requirements, for instance aircraft device equipment would be different from oil manufacturing equipment.

In future, we envision various pre-built asset models available in the catalog to help kick start IoT application for various industry verticals.

Tip - We had explained the concept of abstract data model as part of Solutions Layer section in Chapter 1. The abstract data model is a super set of Asset Data model.

The Asset service consists of an REST API layer, a query engine, and an Apache Cassandra NoSQL graph database. The underlying representation of graph database is available as RDF (Resource Description format) and each data can be represented as a triple (or tuple) of "Subject" , "Predicate" and "Object". The object can be a value or a reference pointing to a Subject. Using RDF provides flexibility for modelling any domain (or any information in the world) as a set of triples. You can design models and relationship and later exploit these facts as part of the application. For instance, you can model a vehicle engine as follows –

Subject	Predicate	Object
/audi/aux566	serialNumber	XXXX-YYYY-ZZZZ
/audi/aux566	manufacturingDate	2015-11-11
/audi/aux566	engineType	XX
/audi/aux566	fuelType	Diesel

/audi/aux566	Torque	XX RPM
/audi/aux566	Power	XX KWT
/audi/aux566	displacement	CMQ

Tip – To know more about RDF and how to model entities and ontology, kindly visit this link - http://naveenbalani.com/index.php/2010/05/introduction-to-semantic-web/. There are ontology models available on the web for various industries, like for automotives you can refer to this link - https://www.w3.org/community/gao/.

Analytics Services

Predix Analytics services provide an environment for running analytics code as a service in Predix Cloud. The Analytics services includes the following set of services -

- Analytics Catalog to catalog your analytics artifacts. The catalog is the central repository of all your analytics artifacts.
- Analytical Orchestration to create orchestration between analytics components.
- Analytics Runtime which provides a scalable runtime for executing analytics orchestration.
- Analytics User Interface to upload your analytics artifacts to Analytics Catalog.

You can develop your analytics code in supported languages such as Python, MATLAB or Java and publish the analytics code to the Analytics Catalog.

Note - The analytics code needs to be developed and deployed as per the Analytics process outlined in the Predix documentation - https://www.predix.io/docs/?r=45293#Qd2kPYb7. Basically you need to package your code and provide configuration file for deployment as per the outlined process.

The Analytics services provide a very good option of leverage existing skills and expertise for building analytics code. Python and MATLAB are widely used in building machine learning algorithms and one can tap into the existing ecosystem to build machine learning algorithms and analytics component based on the industrial use cases.

Apart from your analytics code, there are analytics services offered from ecosystem partners/vendors like Geo-Enhance (by Pitney Bowes) for Geolocation tracking and Anomaly Detection (by ThetaRay) to identify and detect unknown threats and maintenance events to prevent outages. The analytics services from partners and ecosystems would definitely grow over a period of time.

Note – The real value addition offered by any IoT cloud provider would be out of box analytics services for various industries and industry solution templates (refer to solutions layer section in Chapter 1) which can be quickly assembled to create industrial solutions.

The Analytics runtime service provides orchestration of analytic components from the Analytic Catalog and execute them based on rules, timers or events. The orchestration code is specified using the standard BPMN (Business Process Modelling Notation) notation. There is a series of step that needs to be performed for orchestrating and running the analytical code, which is very well documented at Predix website (reference - https://www.predix.io/docs/?r=212627#nQNINP9Q).

Custom Solutions

These are end to end IoT industrial solutions developed using Predix cloud services and third party services. Apart from the above services, Predix cloud provides a bunch of other services that can be used as part of building IoT applications like – user account, authentication and tenant management services, Mobile SDK for building industrial mobile applications, DevOps services or a Dashboard Seed service to setup contextual monitoring application. You can find all the services in the catalog view of Predix website at https://www.predix.io/catalog/

Implementation Overview
Let's design the connected elevator solution we discussed in the second chapter using Predix IoT stack.

Hardware and Connectivity
In this section we would discuss the hardware and connectivity approach for the elevator use case. We will realize the elevator use case using Predix IoT stack through the following phases we described in Chapter 2 - viz. monitoring (which includes asset management), condition maintenance and finally predictive maintenance.

We would not go into the details of each phase again, but only talk about the implementation steps. The manufacturer as part of his connected design exercise adds various new sensors to the existing elevator control unit to realize the requirements as mentioned in Chapter 2. The elevator manufacturer as a first step leverages its existing investment and tries to keep the connectivity and communication protocol between elevator control unit and rest of components same and installs the Predix Machine on the elevator machine controller. The Predix Machine acts as a gateway providing local storage, analytics and filtering of events and also provides secured communication with the Predix Cloud. The Predix Machine component wraps the filtered data into JSON data and sends it over MQTT protocol to Predix Cloud platform. Through the Predix

EdgeManager Web interface, the device is remotely monitored and managed.

Software Implementation Overview

Following are the high level steps that needs to be performed to build the IoT application

1. Generate the Predix Machine OSGI container artifact containing the required features using Predix Machine SDK.
2. Register devices and get access credentials through EdgeManager.
3. Provision devices (elevator control device) through EdgeManager and install the Predix Machine OSGI container from Step 1 on the devices.
4. Create storage services (Create the asset model and store the model and instances using Asset Data service and create Time Series service for storing raw time series data from devices).
5. Configure Message Topics for communication from devices to Cloud and various Cloud services.
6. Create Analytical Code.
7. Deploy Analytics code in Analytics Catalog.
8. Create Analytics Orchestration configuration for the analytical code and execute analytics orchestration using Analytics runtime.
9. Create web dashboards and/or create Mobile applications using Mobile SDK for remote monitoring and management.

Note – We choose to use an example of running elevator machinery 24*7, instead of picking up a complex industrial use case like oil machinery or water management plant. The steps outlined would be pretty much the same as described above with the addition of complexities around integration with existing industrial devices using protocols like ModBus or setting up a secured compliant network infrastructure from existing manufacturing plants to Predix Cloud.

The above implementation steps are just one of the approaches for building end to end IoT application. The following shows the connected elevator solution using Predix cloud platform and services.

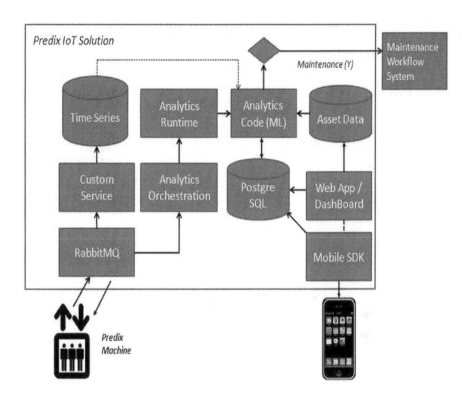

The RabbitMQ service in Predix Cloud receives the data from the connected elevator (controller device) over MQTT protocol. The controller device has Predix Machine software stack installed and uses the MQTT River component to send data to configured topics in RabbitMQ. A custom service is deployed which subscribes to the configured topic and uses the Time Series service to store the time series data. The time series

133

data represents a timestamp and value for each sensors (like temperature, pressure , load etc) which are continuously streamed from the devices, which can be stored and filtered by Predix Machine software component on the elevator control device to do local analysis and/or send it directly to the Predix cloud for analysis. This provides an option of doing simple condition based monitoring and triggering alerts locally and also send only the relevant information over to cloud. The real advantage is that the device can be remotely monitored and the software stack can be updated remotely to add new customizations.

Tip - We could also have used WebSocket protocol instead of MQTT. For supporting WebSocket protocol, we need to use WebSocket River component in Predix Machine software stack to connect to the Predix cloud. The WebSocket River component can also directly post the time series data from devices/sensors to Time Series Gateway component in Predix Cloud.

The Analytics orchestration component is triggered based on message arrival on the specified topic and the required analytic workflow (it can be a single workflow containing your analytical code) is executed by the analytical engine/runtime.

For the elevator use case, 2 analytical components are developed, one for detecting anomaly and other for predictive analytics. The analytics code uses machine learning models and is developed using Python and scikit-learn library. The machine learning model uses time series data, asset data and historical records as inputs for analysis and predictions.

The analytics code is uploaded to Predix Analytics catalog using Predix Analytics User service. Any dependent libraries needs to be specified in a configuration file as per the analytics development process (reference - https://www.predix.io/docs/?r=317800#alaepr9P)

Once the analytic code is tested, you promote it to production state, where it is executed by the analytics runtime.

Tip - As mentioned earlier, the approach of building a machine learning model, whether using Microsoft , Amazon or IBM tools or open source options like Python scikit-learn library remains the same. You build the model and train the model iteratively using the raw data from the connected devices, asset metadata and historical maintenance records. The real challenge in building the model is choosing the right features, cleansing and aggregating the data, applying algorithms, training the model and continuously iterating it to reasonably predict outcome.

Based on the response of analytics service (if maintenance is predicted or required), the maintenance workflow service is triggered. The status is updated in the Postgre SQL database which keeps the track of maintenance activity.

A web dashboard is developed which pulls the data from the data sources (time series, asset data and Postgre SQL database) which shows real-time updates on the entire process and provides monitoring of the assets. The same information is also made available in mobile applications and can also trigger/notify users to take corrective action. The mobile application is developed using Predix Mobile SDK framework, which enables quickly building applications using standards like HTM5 and JavaScript.

This completes an end to end execution cycle using Predix cloud.

Building application with Open Source IoT stack

In this chapter, we will build an IoT stack using open source software. Many vendors are building their own platform for realizing their end to end use cases. Our assessment shows there are at least 100 plus providers providing IoT stack in some form or the other.

Well, the first question that should come to your mind is why you need to build your own IoT stack when there are multiple platform providers providing the same functionality. We list some of the motivations below:

- Start-up providers – The start-up ventures eyes IoT as the hot cake in the market today and are at the forefront of building a cloud platform providing all kinds of cloud services, exploiting various gaps to solve industry specific use cases.
- Hardware/Embedded software manufacturers – Many embedded software manufacturers provides a cloud platform to store the data from the devices, like various OBD vehicle device manufacturers. The data from devices are aggregated in the cloud and analyzed using various tools and techniques.
- Internal evaluation and demos – Software service providers and System Integrators starting their IoT consulting journey or having an embedded software practice and looking at ways to analyze continuous streams of data and build predictive models as service offerings.
- Regulatory compliance - Industries which can't use cloud services due to compliance are building their own in-house platforms for monitoring and condition maintenance activities.

Let's look at our open source IoT stack. We have envisioned this using a popular set of integrated open source software providing high performance, high scalability, and low throughput capabilities.

Open Source IoT Stack

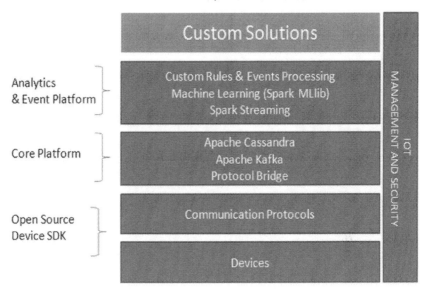

Open Source Device SDKs

The open source IoT platform provides support for wide variety of protocols like MQTT, AXMP, and HTTP protocol. For MQTT, we can leverage the Eclipse-based Paho library for connecting any device to the core platform or open source library like cyclon.js which makes it easier to connect various devices using Node.js. We really liked the cyclone.js library and the extensions provided by the library to support various devices. The following is a snapshot of some of the devices supported by cyclon.js

ARDrone	Arduino	Arduino YUN	Audio
Beaglebone Black	Bebop	BLE	Crazyflie
		Bluetooth	
Digispark	Imp	Intel Galileo	Intel Edison
	electric imp		
Intel IoT Analytics	Joystick	Keyboard	Leap Motion
intel			

Below is the sample code to connect to an analog sensor attached to pin "0" of a device, read the values and transmit the data to the cloud platform using MQTT protocol. It is just 20 lines of code.

```
var Cylon = require('cylon');
Cylon.robot({
  connections:{
    mqtt:{ adaptor:'mqtt',
host:'mqtt://ourserver:port'},
    arduino:{ adaptor:'firmata', port:'/dev/ttyACM0'}
},
  devices:{
    allimit:{ driver:'mqtt', topic:'llimit',
adaptor:'mqtt'},
    aulimit:{ driver:'mqtt', topic:'ulimit',
adaptor:'mqtt'},
    sensor:{ driver:"analogSensor", pin:0,
upperLimit:900, lowerLimit:100}
},
  work:function(my)
    my.sensor.on("upperLimit",function(val){
```

```
        my.aulimit.publish(val);
});
    my.sensor.on("lowerLimit",function(val){
        my.allimit.publish(val);
});
}
}).start();
```

Protocol Bridge

This service acts as a router or gateway for converting incoming protocols to the protocol supported by the core IoT platform. For instance, if the core platform has Apache Kafka set up to process messages and the client communicates using MQTT, then we could write a MQTT server that will receive the data and convert it into the format that Apache Kafka understands. The protocol bridge takes care of sending messages to Apache Kafka over specified topics and determines which partition the message is to be sent.

Apache Kafka

Apache Kafka service provides us with a highly scalable, low latency, fast and distributed publish-subscribe messaging system.

Apache Kafka was developed at LinkedIn. The following link is an excellent blog which talks about how Kafka was used and what problems it solved at LinkedIn - http://www.confluent.io/blog/stream-data-platform-1/. Though, Kafka was not designed as a typical messaging system, it found its roots in many applications which required high throughput distributed messaging framework.

Similar to any publish-subscribe messaging system; Kafka maintains feeds of messages in categories called topics. Producers publish data to topics and consumers subscribe to topics to read messages. In our case, the publisher is the protocol bridge that posts the messages (data from devices) on specified topics. Topics are further partitioned and replicated across nodes. For the connected car use case, we use the main controller device id (the telematics device id or the hardware device id connected to

OBD port) as the partition id to ensure all messages from the same device id ends up in the same partition.

Kafka can retain messages after the specified time interval has elapsed, unlike other messaging systems which delete messages as soon as they are consumed. Going through the entire capabilities of Kafka and its working would require a book in itself. We suggest going through the document http://kafka.apache.org/documentation.html which provides an excellent source of information on Apache Kafka.

Cassandra

We use Apache Cassandra for storing the continuous stream of data coming from devices. We create a Kafka consumer which listens to a specified topic, consumes the message and stores the message in one of the Cassandra tables.

We use Cassandra for historical data analysis to gain insights on various usages, aggregations and computations, build correlations, and to develop our machine learning models iteratively for anomaly detection and predictive analytics. For developing machine learning models, we use Spark Core libraries for connecting to our Cassandra tables and perform data transformation and Spark MLlib libraries for developing machine learning models.

Apache Spark Streaming

Apache Spark streaming component from Apache Spark project adds real-time data stream processing and data transformation for further processing by systems. We chose Apache Spark as it's an ultra-fast in-memory data processing framework. It provides a stack of libraries including SQL and DataFrames, MLlib for machine learning, GraphX, and Spark Streaming. Apache Spark streaming supports real-time processing as well as batch updates on top of Spark engine, which makes it the perfect choice for applications which requires responding to real-time events and batch processing via Hadoop jobs for complex data analysis. Apache Spark streaming component provides first class integration with

Apache Kafka using the Spark Stream Kafka module (spark-streaming-kafka_2.10 version was the latest when we tested the integration). Details of integration are available at this link - http://spark.apache.org/docs/latest/streaming-kafka-integration.html. There are two approaches – Receiver based approach which uses Kafka high-level consumer APIs to consume the messages from a specified topic. This is the old way and requires some workaround to ensure there is no data loss during failures. The other approach is using a direct approach which periodically queries Kafka for the latest offsets in each topic + partition and uses the offset ranges to process data in batches. We have used direct approach for integration and recommend using the same. Once integrated, the streams of data start flowing in Apache Spark Steaming layer, where you can do real-time transformation, filtering and store the data for further analysis or invoke machine learning models (like streaming linear regression).

Apache Spark MLlib

Apache Spark MLlib service is used to build machine learning models or combine multiple machine learning models using a standardized API. Building a machine learning models requires a series of step as discussed earlier –like cleansing and transformation, creating feature vectors, correlation, splitting up data in training and test sets, selecting algorithms for building up required models (prediction, classification, regression, etc.) and iteratively training the model for required accuracy. Typically multiple tools are required to carry out the tasks describe earlier and using Spark APIs and ML libraries everything can be developed iteratively in a single environment.

Custom Rules and Events

For custom rules and events, we create custom application code which is executed as part of the spark streaming flow and trigger's the required action based on the incoming data. Apache Zeppelin project can be used to quickly build an interactive data analytics dashboard. Zeppelin has built-in support for Spark integration and SparkSQL. The project is under incubation and evolving.

Implementation Overview

The implementation steps of realizing the connected car or elevator use case using the open source IoT stack is pretty much the same that we described earlier for IoT stacks from Microsoft, Amazon and IBM, and it's just a matter of replacing services provided by these vendors with open source offerings described above. Though we did not design a complete IoT stack, as we left out the device management capabilities, it still provides a decent perspective of building an end-to-end IoT solution using open source products. The device management and security aspect requires developing custom components to meet the requirements. We leave this as an exercise for you to bring out the best of open source platforms and envision a complete IoT stack.

IoT Comparison chart

To summarize, we have listed the below table showing how various offerings and services maps to the Enterprise IoT stack.

Note –For digital edition, if you have difficulty viewing the table, switch to landscape mode or visit http://enterpriseiotbook.com/compare-iot-stack

---

Platforms ->	Microsoft	IBM	Amazon	Open Source	Predix
Device SDK	Azure IoT Device SDK, Connect TheDots.io	IBM IoTF Client Library, IoTF Device recipes, Paho Library	Device SDK for AWS IoT	Paho Library , Cyclon.js and many other options	Predix Machine
Protocol	HTTP,	MQTT	MQTT,	MQTT,	MQTT,

Supported	AMQP MQTT		HTTP	AMQP, HTTP etc.	Web Socket, HTTPs
Core platform – Database option	Document DB, Storage (high performance tables, blobs), Microsoft SQL	MongoDB, Cloudant NoSQL, Object Storage, Informix Time Series etc.	Amazon Dynamo DB, Amazon Redshift	Cassandra (or alternatives like MongoDB)	Asset Data, Time Series, Redis, Postgre SQL, Blobstore
Analytics platform – Real-time Streaming	Microsoft Stream Analytics	IoT Real-Time Insights, IBM Streaming Analytics	Amazon Kinesis	Apache Spark Streaming	Analytics Runtime
Analytics platform – Machine Learning	Azure ML	Predictive Analytics service (on Bluemix) + SPP Modeler (offline)	Amazon Machine Learning	Apache Spark MLlib	Custom Analytics Support (Python, Java, MATLAB)
Alerts and Event handling	Notification Hubs, PowerBI	Embeddable Reporting, IBM Push Notifications	AWS Lambda, Amazon Quick Sight, Amazon Simple Notification Service	Custom, Zeppelin (Dashboards) etc.	Mobile SDK, Dash board Seed

As mentioned earlier, there are various other complementary services offered by IBM, Amazon, Microsoft and Predix that could be leveraged and used in an IoT solution, like caching, geo-spatial locations, mobile push events etc. There might be many more components which could be used in the above stack, but we listed only those services that provide end-to-end integration in the IoT stack.

From the strategy perspective all platform providers have the same strategy of providing a set of services to enable development of scalable IoT applications. Clearly, just providing the platform would not provide any unique capability and we would see lot of tie-ups and partnership from device manufacturers to network providers, open source adopters to start-up's providing innovative solutions. Apart from partnerships, the real requirement is to develop and provide end to end industry solutions on top of the IoT stack as a set of offerings which can be customized based on requirements. For instance, design model of the services used with a connected car solution should not change across car manufacturer. The only thing that would change is device library that is fitted in the car (telematics device) or installed via the OBD port.

Summary

In this chapter, our intent was to present a neutral view on how to use cloud services provided by various cloud providers to build IoT applications and even build one based on open source software. The strategy adopted by all the cloud providers is to provide a set of services which can be composed to develop IoT applications (for that matter any application). Choosing one cloud vendor as opposed to other depends on various requirements and it's outside the scope of the book.

Wrap Up

In this book, our intent was to provide a first of a kind reference on how to get started on building Enterprise IoT applications.

We believe the concepts and content laid down in the book would be a useful resource to build any IoT application and be a part of your IoT journey. As we wrap up the first edition of the book, we have already started to work on the second edition to cover more IoT platforms and end to end solutions.

We would like to hear from you. For questions, suggestions, queries and future revisions on the book, please reach out to us at http://enterpriseiotbook.com/

Appendix

Cognitive IoT

This bonus chapter provides a short introduction to Cognitive IoT and provides my vision and architecture for a Cognitive IoT solution.

This chapter assumes you have gone through the Enterprise IoT stack and Cognitive Computing concepts as described in Chapter 1.

Cognitive Internet of Things is about enabling current IoT technologies with human-like intelligence.

Cognitive systems in the context of IoT would play a key role in future. Imagine 10 years down the line where every piece of a system is connected to the internet and probably an integral part of everyday lives and information being shared continuously, how you would like to interact with these smart devices which surround you. It would be virtually talking to smart devices and devices responding to you based on your action and behaviour.

Let's take an example of a cognitive IoT application. I have taken a very simple example to get the technology and benefits across.

1. I step out of my home and the home electricity turns into a power saver mode.
2. I step into the car and the car recognizes me.
3. My car seats are automatically adjusted.
4. My favorite music station is set and the play list is started.
5. Aggregated news for the day is available and tailored for me on my dashboard and read it out by the dashboard device. If I am travelling, weather forecast and news related to the place I am travelling is available as an add-on.
6. As I pass by malls, my car reminds to purchase stuff.
7. I sync my digital cart and get my purchases quickly. No need to move around, find things and put it to a physical cart.

8. I come back to my car, I start interacting with the Car in Natural human language instead of typing in numbers and searching for things.
9. I ask for good places for lunch which I haven't visited. Based on my past experiences and cuisine preference, ratings from third party sites, a set of recommendations are provided. I choose one of them.
10. GPS devices are synced up based on my response and direction's changed.
11. An alternative route is automatically selected based on traffic sensors and weather condition which the GPS device is subscribed to.
12. I have lunch, I don't need to carry cards, I am being recognized. The best credit card (after checking available offers for that restaurant) from my digital wallet is automatically selected and used for the payment. Welcome to smart cashless transactions.
13. I come back home, lights are back up again, all devices started
14. I say "good night", lights are dimmed and tell my clock to wake me up at 7:00 am after checking my flight status.

As you see in the above example, the real value is derived from how data from sensors are used as part of the broader ecosystem and how cognitive capabilities and learning are used to provide value added services. This is not programmed but learned over time. For instance, the connected car over a period of time should also provide recommendations on how to improve the mileage based on your driving patterns.

In future, you should be able to speak to devices through tweets, spoken words, gestures and devices would be able to understand the context and respond accordingly. For instance, a smart device as part of connected home would react differently as compared to devices in a connected car.

For a connected home, a cognitive IoT system can learn from you, set things up for you based on your patterns and movements, be it waking you up at the right time, start your coffee vending machines, sending you a WhatsApp message to start washing machine if you missed to start it based on your routine or take care of the home lighting system based on your family preferences. Imagine putting a smart controller and set of devices around your home, which observes you over a period of time and start making intelligent decisions on Day 10 and continuously learn from you and your family interactions.

This is one of the areas where we would see a lot of innovation and investment happening in future and would be a key differentiator for connected products and extension to one's digital lives.

Next, we will look at how to realize the Cognitive IoT architecture.

The architecture of a connected word

Let's start with a high level view of an IoT Cognitive Systems Architecture. The real value of IoT applications is realized by enabling them as part of existing applications and higher value-added services to create new innovative business solutions.

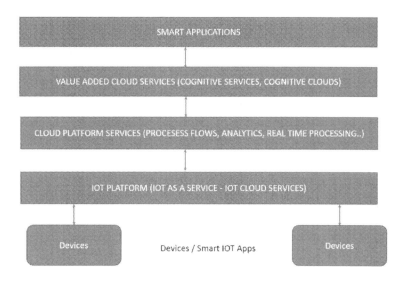

We have described the capabilities of an Enterprise IoT Stack in Chapter 1.

While existing IoT platforms provide a kick start, there is a need for a higher level of abstraction for devices, protocols, lifecycle management and deployment in the near future.

With respect to IoT protocols, during the course of the book, we talked about standards like MQTT & CoAP which are better suited for constrained environments than the standard web protocol (HTTP) and choosing a protocol depends on your application needs. There are evolving proposals like HPACK – Header Compression for HTTP/2 for compressing header fields in the requests which can be looked at for constrained devices. The point is with existing or new protocols, the IoT platform and sender/receiver needs to be aware of the protocol.

Also supporting a new device/hardware configuration requires an effort to make a set of libraries (device SDKs) available which helps to get started on the device. The programming model supported for each device would be different. Also, management of billions of devices, life-cycle, code updates and firmware upgrades are still to be solved at large.

Secondly with devices being an integral part of our lives in a connected world, I envision a much stronger interconnect not just between machines, but also machine to human interaction and the whole cognitive aspects around it, where machines and humans (as well as machine to machine interaction) interacts using natural language, understand the context (based on the domains where IoT is applied), learns over a period of time from your behavioural patterns and suggest recommendations.

With the above aspects in mind, I propose the following architecture -

- An abstract communication protocol for devices.
- A Twitter-based architecture model for IoT with sophisticated event-driven capabilities.
- A deployment model similar to container solutions like Docker for IoT.

A New Cognitive IoT Architecture

Don't you think it would be cool if a device can tweet about their status using natural language (instead of signals) and followers could pick up their status and do the next level of processing or take no action?

How about a car engine oil component communicating #change oil, which is followed by your maintenance engine guy which comes and changes the car oil? Here individual components can be followed by device or humans who may end up taking a corrective action.

How about you communicating to device #Wakeup at 7:00 after checking PNR #XXX or once you start your car, you get all reports of your car components in your dashboard –

#oilcc ok

#cartyrefront1 ok

#cartyrefront2 ok

#cartyrefront3 ok

#cartyrefront4 less by 2%

#enginecc ok

How about you asking question about your car via an iTweet –

@nb -> what is the mileage @xyz so far.

How about your car learning from your behaviour and data and providing suggestions via iTweets –

@xyz -> @nb you can improve the mileage by the following...

The implementations and deployment can vary. You can have a private community to receive/restrict messages and follow various public communities (weather forecasts etc) to utilize the data and act on it.

With respect to protocol, the application/device doesn't need to worry about underlying protocols (MQTT, CoAP etc.) and communicate via the highest level of abstraction -> the natural language. The device can be equipped to take care of underlying implementations or hand off all communications to a controller (or edge/device/intelligent gateway) which decides the next course of action and provides the next step to these devices. The device itself may not be equipped to handle context, understanding languages and context and have the lowest power consumption and totally rely on the controller which communicates the right signals for devices to carry out.

Even a simple curl like implementation can be use by device to send messages and bulk of processing happening in controllers, like

#devicexx icurl "engine being shut down"

Note - curl is a tool to transfer data from or to a server using supported protocols. The tool is designed to work without user interaction.

As we deploy IoT in different domains, the devices, controllers and underlying implementation would be well equipped to handle languages and context for that domain. The controller can leverage cognitive services to understand the language and the context in that domain. A connected home would use a different terminology than a connected car.

This is just one aspect, how about a private WhatsApp group for your devices, sharing their status and taking corrective action or a social community of connected cognitive devices, interconnected with your actual social profiles. Gartner predicts *Customer experience innovation* is one of Top Trends for 2015 and coming up with innovate solutions would be a key going forward.

I have talked about the consumer perspective only, but the same concepts can be extended to any service lifecycle of an object in any industry, right from its inception to its predictive maintenance as described in manufacturing use cases earlier and using this information as part of an existing application or new value added solutions to create innovate products and make lives safer and simpler.

Docker for IoT (Deployment, Upgrades and more)

Docker is an open platform for developers and sysadmins to build, ship, and run distributed applications, whether on laptops, data center VMs, or the cloud.

As we look at developing new IoT-based applications, deploying it to millions of devices and supporting multiple hardware configurations, rolling out new changes, we need a container technology like docker to take care of many such challenges. Docker is gaining momentum as it solves a key problem. I have seen some early traction already and companies are coming up with solutions to deploy docker containers to constraint devices. Imagine you can use your existing skills like Node.js, python to build out applications and deploy to connected device. Also, roll out and upgrades mean changing docker images, which would make it a whole lot easier. Watch out for this space as we see new technology enablers which would make it easier for rapid IoT deployments.

Hope this short introduction gave you enough insights and food for thought for a connected world. Stay tuned, exciting times ahead.

32426654R00091

Made in the USA
San Bernardino, CA
05 April 2016